Contents

Acknowledgements

We are indebted to Falmer Press Ltd for permission to reproduce an extract from an article by L. Measor pp 178/179 *Curriculum Practice* edited by Hammersley & Hargreaves (1983).

Series introduction

Sociology in Focus aims to provide an up-to-date, coherent coverage of the main topics that arise on an introductory course in sociology. While the intention is to do justice to the intricacy and complexity of current issues in sociology, the style of writing has deliberately been kept simple. This is to ensure that the student coming to these ideas for the first time need not become lost in what can appear initially as jargon.

Each book in the series is designed to show something of the purpose of sociology and the craft of the sociologist. Throughout the different topic areas the interplay of theory, methodology and social policy have been highlighted, so that rather than sociology appearing as an unwieldy collections of facts, the student will be able to grasp something of the process whereby sociological understanding is developed. The format of the books is broadly the same throughout. Part one provides an overview of the topic as a whole. In part two the relevant research is set in the context of the theoretical, methodological and policy issues. The student is encouraged to make his or her own assessment of the various arguments, drawing on the statistical and reference material provided both here and at the end of the book. The final part of the book contains both statistical material and a number of 'Readings'. Questions have been provided in this section to direct students to analyse the materials presented in terms of both theoretical assumptions and methodological approaches. It is intended that this format should enable students to exercise their own sociological imaginations rather than to see sociology as a collection of universally accepted facts, which just have to be learned.

While each book in the series is complete within itself, the similarity of format ensures that the series as a whole provides an integrated and balanced introduction to sociology. It is intended that the text can be used both for individual and classroom study, while the inclusion of the variety of statistical and documentary materials lend themselves to both the preparation of essays and brief seminars.

PART 1

Introduction and overview

1 Introduction

All intellectual enterprises have their own history. Areas of study like the sociology of education can be traced as they develop and change over time. Theories rise and fall, gaining and then losing popularity. Techniques of research and topics of special interest also become fashionable for a time and are then replaced by new concerns. This does not mean that the out-of-fashion work disappears entirely. Intellectual traditions in the social sciences can be thought of as being rather like stratified rock, each new phase, each new fashion, is sedimented into place, making its own contribution to the whole endeavour. Indeed there are occasions when almost totally forgotten ideas or theoretical positions are reasserted. But this sort of conception of a discipline or area of study needs to be treated with some caution. First, it is a mistake to think of such changes and developments over time as somehow independent of the men and women who write the theories and do the research. Changes arise from the conflicts and disputes between people holding different positions. The intellectual history of the sociology of education is also an account of the work and commitment of a relatively small group of theorists and researchers. Second, it is also a mistake to view the changing pattern of ideas in an area of study like the sociology of education as independent of the social context, both political and economic, in which it is set. Changes in the political climate, government policies, and economic events all make an impact upon the prevailing body of ideas and theories.

Since its beginnings in the 1930s the sociology of education in Britain has been concerned above all with the analysis of the relationship between 'social class and educational opportunity'.

Thus a great deal of the research done has taken as its focus the description or explanation of social class differences in access to and achievement in education. This tradition is often referred to as 'political arithmetic' (a name taken from a book published in 1938, edited by Lancelot Hogben). During the 1950s this approach was established as the basis for British sociology of education, particularly as a result of work done on education and social mobility at the London School of Economics (and replicated in 1980 in the study *Origins and Destinations,* see pp.73–74). The two best-known proponents of this approach were Jean Floud and A. H. Halsey, whose work did much to gain acceptance for the sociology of education as a valid and reputable area of study in British universities.

Much of the impetus for this early research came from a belief that the existing pattern of education was both wasteful and unfair. Wasteful inasmuch as valuable resources in the form of human talent and intelligence were being lost to the nation as a result of the separate system of grammar schools and secondary moderns. Unfair because in virtually all of the studies done it was pupils from working-class homes who were underrepresented in grammar schools, in staying on at school after the minimum leaving age, in going on to higher education, etc. The researchers were attempting to use their work to address and influence policy-making, and the attack on inequality mounted during this period played an important part in the political struggle over the organisation of secondary schooling, that of selective versus comprehensive. Floud and Halsey certainly gained a hearing within the Labour Party and did much to lay the foundations for the eventual adoption of a policy of comprehensive education. The research done in the early 1950s clearly demonstrated that while the 1944 Education Act had had a notable effect upon the pattern of entry into grammar schools, 'class-chances' for entry were still weighted heavily in favour of children from middle-class homes.

In Table 1.1 we can see that children from the working class were much less successful in taking up places in the expanded grammar school and university systems after the Second World War than were those from other social classes. While the percentage of working-class pupils going into selective schooling does increase, the percentage of middle-class pupils increases even more. The gap between the two increased. But

Table 1.1

Changes in the social distribution of educational opportunity. Secondary and university education of boys reaching the age of eleven before and after the Second World War, in England and Wales.

		Percentage attending		
		Working class	Others	All
1931–40	Independent efficient or grammar	9·8	38·9	14·7
	University	1·7	8·5	3·7
1946–51	Independent efficient or grammar	14·5	48·5	23·0
	University	1·6	19·2	5·6

Source: Floud, J. 'Some Class Factors in Educational Achievements', in Craft, M. (Ed) Family, Class and Education, London, Longman (1970) p.37.

there were also significant differences in attainment within the working class. Children of unskilled or semi-skilled fathers fared particularly badly.

The question which needed to be answered was what caused these difference in social class achievement. Three immediate possibilities presented themselves. First, it could have been a straightforward matter that middle–class children are intellectually superior and that differences in measured IQ are accurate reflections of differences in 'educability'. This argument was put forward by some psychologists in the 1950s and has had a recent revival in the work of Eysenck. Eysenck argues that:

> For many years IQ tests were instrumental in securing a better education for (the bright working–class child) than they would otherwise have been able to obtain; the elimination of such tests by left–wing governments is still one of the least intelligible actions taken in the name of advancing the status of the deprived child . . . For all those who wish genuinely to restore to bright working–class children the best opportunities for an

education appropriate to their talents, the restoration of IQ
tests to their rightful place seems the best, if not the only way.
  Eysenck, H.J. *The Inequality of Man,* London, Temple Smith,
                                                    (1973) pp. 224–5.

Second, it could be that IQ testing is inherently innaccurate and
socially biased against the working-class child. This argument
was certainly put forward. And the overall validity of IQ testing
as an effective predictor of academic performance has been
seriously called into question (see Eysenck, H.J. versus Kamin, L.
(1981).) Also, it was found that practice with tests could increase
scores by as much as ten points and that errors of between 10 and
13 per cent might be involved in allocating children to secondary
schools on the basis of IQ testing. However, the sociology of
education took its future direction from a third area of possible
investigation.

The consistent tendency of working-class or manual workers'
children to perform less well in school, and to leave school
sooner than the children of non-manual workers even when
they are of similar ability, calls for explanation, and it has
seemed reasonable to look for that explanation in the experiences and attitudes of the working-class family.
  Banks, O. *The Sociology of Education,* London, Batsford,
                                                    (1968) pp. 61–62.

Until the late 1960s research on social class inequalities in
education focused almost exclusively on the relationships between home background and educational achievement. Initially
it was the material environment that was explored. Factors such
as poor housing, over-crowding, poverty and malnutrition were
implicated in working-class under-achievement. But it was not
long before more subtle and sophisticated accounts began to
emerge. A whole series of studies were aimed at demonstrating
the value differences which existed between working-class and
middle-class parents. Working-class pupils were said to be
unable to 'defer gratification', while middle-class pupils were
brought up in a milieu which stressed 'status achievement' and
individual competition. These sorts of concerns led on naturally
to research into child-rearing and the socialisation process
within the family. Attempts were made to link different types of
parental behaviour to high and low levels of achievement

motivation. But in this area findings were often contradictory and causal relationships were difficult to establish. Many such studies were certainly able to identify differences in child-rearing practices between the social classes. Few if any could actually demonstrate that these differences were directly related to achievement motivation scores and thence to school performance.

Perhaps the most potent element in all of this research is that associated with Basil Bernstein. Begining in the late 1950s Bernstein published a series of papers which explored the thesis that certain social factors critical to the socialisation process within the family are related to and affect the child's linguistic performance. Further, that these differences in linguistic performances, dubbed speech codes by Bernstein, prepare children more or less well for school learning. In the minds of many readers and disseminators of Bernstein's work his analysis reinforced a conception of working-class language and culture as somehow inadequate, and a poor preparation for school. For many teachers it provided a powerful and appealing explanation for differences in classroom performance, and the theory of codes did much to reinforce the emerging 'deficit model' of the working-class child. Working-class pupils came to be seen as culturally and linguistically deprived and in need therefore of 'compensatory education'. To a great extent the work on family background and school achievement (some of these studies are discussed in more detail in Chapter 2) remained inconclusive, achieving little in the way of precise insight into the way in which different background factors interrelate to raise or depress school performance. And perhaps one of the most significant factors in the enormous concentration of intellectual energy is that it neglected almost entirely the child's experience inside the school. It tended to be assumed that the school was a more or less neutral institution within which social class differences in culture, attitudes and motivation were played out. It was taken for granted in this type of research that pupils carried with them into school a fixed set of cultural resources and personal abilities which remained with them throughout their school careers. Indicators of social class differences in home background were applied at one end and measures of difference in attainment taken at the other. The school itself, apart from some rather ill-defined notions about middle-class bias, remained unresearched, a set of unknowns, undisturbed by the harsh gaze of the researcher's eye.

This state of affairs began to change with the publication in 1967 of Hargreaves' study *Social Relations in a Secondary School* and in 1970 of C. Lacey's *Hightown Grammar* (Manchester University Press, Manchester). Both these studies were part of a research initiative based at the University of Manchester, which sought to extend the methods of anthropological research to the investigation of the major institutions of modern society. The books are both case-studies of single schools, Hargreaves' a secondary modern, and Lacey's a grammar. They took the investigation of social class and educational inequality inside the school to examine the effects of both the formal organisation, specifically the systems of streaming used to group the pupils for teaching purposes, and the informal peer group pressures experienced by the pupils. The two studies demonstrated the ways in which in-school processes could exacerbate or in some cases modify the effects of differences in pupils' home backgrounds, and they mark the begining of a major shift in emphasis in the focus of educational research, away from the home to the school. But more than this these two studies also played their part in a revolution in theory and method in the sociology of education.

The use of participant observation techniques and concepts of explanation drawn from symbolic interactionism went directly against the prevailing orthodoxies (see Fig. 1.1).

To be sure, much of the sociology of education done in Britian up to the mid-1960s was only weakly informed by theory, the emphasis was on empirical description through the accumulation of statistical data. In sociology generally structural functionalist theory (see Fig 1.2) was dominant and insofar as it impinged upon the sociology of education it tended to reinforce a concern with the 'macrosociological study of educational institutions'.

Hargreaves and Lacey did a great deal to demonstrate the possibilities and worthwhileness of an alternative approach, their focus being on micro-sociological processes, person-to-person interaction, rather than grand social theory and statistical generalisations based on large representative populations. Their ground-breaking work was quickly and powerfully reinforced by the publication in 1971 of a collection of essays under the title *Knowledge and Control,* edited by M.F.D. Young. This collection

Fig. 1.1   Symbolic interactionism.

Symbolic interactionism derives from the work of George Herbert Mead. The primary focus is on the individual social actor. Individuals are taken to be involved in active interpretation of their social world, making decisions about how to act from alternative options and possibilities. The key concept is the *self*, the developing social aspect of the person. People change, adapt and respond through the self and the self is also the mechanism through which they interpret and make sense of the social environment, always taking into account the actions and projects of others. Their behaviour is not determined either by social conditioning or psychological drives but is the product of construction and choice. Actors bring with them into a situation a unique set of previous experiences, expectations and intentions. Thus, social settings are the outcome of negotiation, compromise and conflict between the definitions and concerns of different actors. It follows that in order to study and understand social life the researcher must try to share and understand the meanings and interpretations of individual actors and social groups. That means being alongside them, talking to them and observing them – participant observation. The emphasis of symbolic interaction research is usually micro-sociological, the study of social processes in specific settings, e.g. a school, a hospital, a classroom, a gang, a neighbourhood.

drew heavily on phenomenological theory (see Fig. 1.3) and the work of Alfred Schutz, and it provided the basis of what came to be known as the 'new' sociology of education.

Young proposed that the sociology of education should take as its primary concern the political character of educational knowledge – the school curriculum – through research into the ways in which it is controlled. Educational knowledge, Young argued, is socially constructed and as such it is a reflection of certain political interests. The whole emphasis of the collection being to call into question the whole range of shared understandings that provide the basis for what counts as education.

Fig. 1.2   Structural functionalism.
Structural functionalism is outlined in some detail in Chapter 2. It is identified in particular with Talcott Parsons. It takes as its primary focus the whole society and the maintenance of social integration. Parsons in particular identifies the continuance of the society with the successful internalisation of basic norms and values in individual personalities and the development of particular social organisations which operate to achieve this socialisation process – the family, the church, the education system. Individuals learn to behave according to the social position that they will take up in the society, behaviour is constrained and formed according to established 'expectations'. Here the individual is very much the passive product of the society. All action and social organisation are to be understood ultimately in terms of the functions they perform for the society. The fulfilment of these functions ensures continuity and stability.

... sociological questions for research in education (or politics or industry for that matter) can only be posed by not accepting the ideas and institutions of the system that those involved in it are constrained to take as granted. This is true for ... categories like teacher and pupil or even what counts as education, ability and achievement.

Young, M.F.D. 'On the politics of educational knowledge', *Economy and Society*, 1(2) (1972) p.56.

Suddenly a range of areas previously untouched by research-teacher–pupil interaction, labelling of pupil deviance, the definition of school knowledge, teachers' definitions of ability – were opened up for scrutiny. The sociology of education acquired a whole new agenda of issues and a new body of theory and concepts to apply to them. A new generation of researchers were spending their time not in constructing and piloting questionnaires and acquiring the necessary statistical techniques to process their data, but were sitting in classrooms and staffrooms, interviewing teachers and pupils, and taking away notebooks full of observations and briefcases full of tape cassettes. The

Fig. 1.3 Phenomenology

Phenomenology is often confused with or identified with interactionism but in a number of ways it is distinct and different. It derives from the work of Alfred Schutz and is concerned with the taken-for-granted knowledge and social assumptions which organise and constrain the ways in which individuals act in the course of their everyday lives. Schutz's work was aimed at producing a systematic account of the common-sense world as social reality, what he calls the 'life-world'. He is often described as being concerned with 'meanings' but that is only partly true. Phenomenology is not really concerned with what people think, but the ways in which their thoughts are unknowingly structured and organised, through the use of typifications, recipe knowledge, relevance structures, idealisations, and finite provinces of meaning. What Schutz's work did was to alert sociologists of education to the necessity of attending to the common-sense knowledge of individual actors and the ways in which they make sense of their immediate social world.

result of all this was that the methodological dominance of positivism (reliant on quantitative techniques), and the theoretical dominance of functionalism, were both successfully challenged and overturned.

However, the new approaches were not without critics of their own. Early studies were attacked for their lack of proper concern for research method and a tendency to focus on trivial aspects of school life, and in some cases their 'sentimental egalitarianism'. Researchers in the 'political arithmetic' tradition bemoaned the lack of policy relevance, and the difficult and obfuscatory language employed by some of the 'new' writers tended to alienate their readers. On the other hand the work done by Hargreaves and Lacey, and later Woods, Ball and others was addressed to issues within the immediate concern of teachers – classroom management, pupil deviance, innovatory teaching methods – and was accessible to them in ways that previous research had never been. 'Interactionism speaks more clearly to practitioners than do some forms of sociology with higher degrees of abstraction and wider, system-related, concerns' (Woods, P.E. *Sociology and the School,* London, Routledge and Kegan Paul, (1983)).

Interactionism is concerned with the meanings and interpretations of individual actors as the basic building blocks of sociological analysis. Phenomenology was used as a critical tool for uncovering taken-for-granted conceptions of educational practice. Both have parallels in the social and political movements of the 1960s. The hippy phenomenon, the increased interest in transcendental religions and hallucinogenic drugs all involved celebration of 'the individual' and challenge to established norms and beliefs. In education too, students and radical teachers were demanding an end to authoritarian forms of teaching, more individual freedom of choice and greater participation in the decision-making. In the newly-founded comprehensive schools, for a brief period at least, the onus was on innovation. Traditional structures and forms of social relationship were being broken down, the past was viewed as no longer relevant. Curriculum projects were being designed to increase pupil choice as to what and how they should learn. In primary schools 'informal' progressive teaching methods were replacing the existing emphasis on the 'transmission' of knowledge. Some writers went further and argued for the need to de-school, to abolish the institution as we know it altogether. The essential point here is that change seemed eminently possible. History and structure appeared not to be inevitable constraints. The economic situation allowed for increased spending on education, although the Labour governments of the late 1960s did face a number of financial crises and a growing rate of inflation.

In the early 1970s the political and economic climate began to shift again. In educational circles the impression of widespread innovation in schools and dramatic television pictures of student demonstrators taking to the streets to make their point, stimulated the beginnings of a political backlash which was to gain momentum through the 1970s. In 1969 the first in a series of Black Papers, *The Fight for Education* (Cox, C.B. and Dyson, A.E. (eds), London, The Critical Quaterly Society) was published. While this pamphlet was dominated by concerns about the 'collapse of community' in higher education it also contained the first in a series of trenchant attacks on the idea of comprehensive education, egalitarianism and 'progressive teaching methods'. These attacks were articulated through a number of basic themes which were echoed and reinforced in the remaining Black Papers and quickly taken up in the popular press and television. Three themes were to the forefront: 'declining standards of education', 'the political indoctrination of pupils by radical teachers' and 'classroom violence and increasing juvenile delinquency'. The short period of optimism in education, sometimes called 'the progressive consensus' was coming to an end. Furthermore, the connection between the provision of more education and increasing national income and productivity, 'human capital theory', was also being seriously challenged. With the onset of the world oil crisis in 1974, high inflation and rising unemployment, the question being asked in virtually all western countries was whether they could afford to go on spending more and more money on education.

Again it is possible to draw parallels with changes going on in the sociology of education. The interactionist position was coming under criticism from a new direction. A series of influential neo-Marxist studies (see Fig. 1.4) published in the mid-1970s (Sharp and Green's *Education and Social Control* (1975), Bowles and Gintis' *Schooling in Capitalist America* (1976), and Willis' *Learning to Labour* (1977)) reasserted a structural analysis of educational processes. In doing so they highlighted what they saw as the failure of interactionism to escape from its preoccupation with the micro-sociological arena of face-to-face interaction and individual interpretations.

> The sociologist should . . . go beyond the phenomenological preoccupation with human meanings and the actions with which they are logically connected. To stop there would be unnecessarily limiting and not enable the analyst to evolve any movement beyond the purely descriptive or illustrative level of inquiry.
>
> Sharp and Green (1975) p.45.

Significantly, however, in many cases the arguments put forward by the neo-Marxists attempt to build upon the achievements of the interactionist position rather than reject entirely the interactionist enterprise. Sharp and Green for example were concerned to take seriously the meanings of the actors they studied but go on to argue that:

Fig.1.4   Neo-Marxism

Neo-Marxism is so called because it involves both an updating of Marx's original ideas and their combination with ideas from other theories. The terms Marxian and Marxist have been suggested to distinguish between Marx's original work and later adaptations and developments. For our purposes neo-Marxism represents a view which gives considerable autonomy to the education system, releasing it from direct subordination to the economy, although still related to it in important ways. Education is taken to be a site of contradictions and struggle. Progressive and reactionary groups are at work attempting to influence or control the education process, and schooling is not passively and unquestioningly accepted by all of its participants, teachers or pupils. While schools are primarily involved in the process of reproducing the statuses and opportunities of different social class groups this reproduction is sometimes untidy and incomplete, creating mismatches between pupil expectations and objective economic conditions. Neo-Marxists also diverge from the orthodox methods of Marxism – historical materialism – exploring and analysing the actions and perspectives of individual social actors and particular social groups and attempting to relate these to processes of social control and social reproduction. Compared with interactionism and structural-functionalism, neo-Marxism is not a precise theoretical position, rather it describes a whole set of diverse theorists and researchers who have attempted to rework or reorient basic Marxian ideas and concepts.

Without a careful analysis of the actor's situation and the kind of constraints on action imposed, there may be a danger of overemphasising or reifying a one-sided and partial view of man (sic) stressing 'freedom' and 'creativity' instead of seeing these as themselves social products of particular kinds of circumstances. (p.59.)

And it is also important to note that Sharp and Green, and Willis employed techniques of participant observation in their research, drawing on the experience and expertise of interactionism. What these researchers attempted to do was to establish links between the micro-sociological processes of the school and the classroom and the macro-sociological structures of capitalist society. Each, in different ways, portrays the school as playing its part in reproducing the social and technical relations of capitalism. That is to say, they see schooling as a way of making the sons and daughters of working-class parents into a new generation of workers who will unquestioningly accept their role in the labour force. This is neatly summed up in the sub-title of Willis' book, 'How working class kids get working class jobs'. (We will look more closely at the substance of these studies in Chapter 2.)

More recently some interactionists have sought to respond to the neo-Marxist challenge by developing their own concepts to establish links between the macro and micro levels of analysis. There is an ongoing dialogue between the proponents of the two positions, sometimes acrimonious but often constructive. Synthesis has been one of the prevailing themes in the sociology of education in the past few years.

From one point of view then the 1970s can be seen as a decade of debate between structuralist and interactionist positions in the sociology of education. However, there is another field of major development in both theory and research which has made at least as significant an impact on the sociology of education and which also in some ways bridges the gap between micro and macro. That is feminism (see Fig. 1.5). It can be argued that feminism stands in its own right as a major analytical perspective.

Responding to the women's liberation movement and an increasing awareness of women's issues in all facets of social life, sociologists have begun to take on board sex and gender as primary analytical categories to set alongside the perennial concern with social class. Women sociologists have been critical of the way in which the social sciences have been dominated by a male point of view. They point to the 'invisibility' of women in most research and the tendency for male researchers to assume that findings based on studies of men can be generalised to women. Thus in the sociology of education researchers have begun to explore the ways in which schooling plays its part in perpetuating the subordination of women within society. Stu-

Fig. 1.5   Feminism

Feminism is not a social theory directly equivalent to Marxism or functionalism, rather it is an analytical perspective and an agenda of issues. The primary concern is with exploring and explaining the position of women in society, in particular their subordination to and oppression by men. In some cases the oppression of women is identified with, or reduced to, the relations of production under capitalism. Women are socialised to accept positions as domestic labourers, servicing the home and caring for children, while their husbands go out to 'work'. When necessary to the economy women provide a source of cheap labour for industry but they are frequently subjected to inferior wages and conditions of service. Schooling plays its part in teaching girls to accept their future position primarily as wives and mothers as being natural and inescapable. They learn that they are inferior to boys in crucial areas of personality and ability (e.g. temperamental, lacking in objectivity, squeamish, submissive, indecisive). Thus school reproduces the established relations between the sexes and a division of labour which disadvantages women. In other words, schools maintain and reproduce the conditions of a patriarchal (male dominated) society. An important distinction here is between sex – the biological basis of male and female differences – and gender – the learned, cultural aspects of masculine and feminine identity. Gender issues are treated fairly briefly in this book, and readers are referred to Madden, P. *Sociology in Focus – Gender,* London, Longman, (1986) for a more detailed treatment.

dies have focused on the classroom, and such things as the unequal distribution of time and attention given by teachers to boys and girls, the curriculum, the ways in which books and materials tend to reproduce stereotypes of women as inferior to men, and those processes which limit women's access to higher education, high status knowledge, and areas of vocational preparation traditionally dominated by men.

Certainly less well developed but nonetheless making itself felt, there is also a movement in the sociology of education to establish race as a basic concept in a similar way. There is a growing body of literature which examines the experience of schooling from the point of view of Asian and West Indian pupils, and attention is being given to the occurrence and perpetuation of racist attitudes in schools. In both cases, race and gender, important contributions have been made by both interactionist and structuralist researchers. Questions of gender and race are relevant both in the attitudes of individual actors and their interactions with one another, and in the basic structures of inequality and discrimination which extend across society as a whole and reproduce patriarchy and racism.

As I suggested earlier, since the early 1970s political attitudes towards education have undergone a profound transformation. The dominant message of the 1970s articulated by both main political parties has been that schools and teachers have somehow failed to take adequate account of, and service the needs of, British industry. It has been claimed that the academic ethos of Britain's schools has actually contributed to a decline of the industrial spirit. In 1975 the Labour government launched the 'Great Debate' on education, which took teachers to task for their lack of accountability to parents and to industrialists. This attack provided a solid platform for the Conservative government of 1979 to begin to restructure the existing relationships between schools and parents and central government. There has been a steady but marked increase in intervention in school matters by agencies of central government (The Department of Education and Science, the Department of Industry and the Manpower Services Commission). And schools have become subject to the same 'market forces' at work in commerce and industry.

Not surprisingly such wide-ranging and significant changes in government policies and school-government relationships have led to a reawakening within the sociology of education of interest in policy-related research and policy analysis, and a small but growing literature on the politics of education. Attempts are being made once again to plot and analyse the effects of government policies on educational opportunity and the social distribution of life chances. More specifically, research is being conducted into the relationship between education and unemployment focusing on educational attainment and patterns of unemployment and on the ways in which schemes like the Youth Opportunities Programme (YOP) and the Youth Training Scheme (YTS) provide access to jobs and affect the attitudes and motivation of the young people who pass through them.

The field of the sociology of education has moved over a thirty year period from a state of theoretical under-development, where one theory and one set of methods predominated, to a current situation of theoretical and methodological plurality. A range of theories compete and coexist offering different kinds of concepts, insights and systems of analysis. Some of these are compatible, others contain assumptions which make them irreconcilable. There is also now a highly-developed division of the area into sub-specialisms. Rather than talk about the sociology of education as a whole it is often necessary to specify the sociology of the curriculum, gender, schooling and race, teacher-pupil interaction, the school as an organisation, the politics of education, etc. In the following chapter we will look more closely at some of these concerns, although in a book of this size a fully comprehensive review is impossible. Where it is useful to do so I have indicated further reading and some activities and exercises are included. At this stage it is important that you have begun to have some grasp of the theoretical complexity and scope of the sociological study of education.

PART 2

Sociology and education

2 The changing structure of educational provision

Many of the substantive issues raised in the previous chapter have their origins in the history of educational provision in this country. Matters of educational policy like comprehensive reorganisation, the introduction of vocational education courses and the different school experiences of boys and girls need to be set in their historical context. Very briefly, this chapter is intended to provide that context.

Any review of the history of educational provision in this country will inevitably highlight two basic facts. First that education has, since the earliest days of state involvement, been a matter of serious political contention. Second, that the pattern of educational provision reflects strongly the social class divisions within the country as a whole.

Mass schooling

Mass schooling began in Britain with the passing of the 1870 Education Act. The intention of the Act was to provide elementary schooling (up to 11 years) for children then lacking it, by the establishment of School Boards. These public elementary schools were intended primarily for working–class children and could charge a fee of up to 9d (3.75p) a week. School attendance however was not made compulsory until 1880, and tuition was not provided free in most schools until 1891. Interpretations of the reasons for the passing of the 1870 Act differ. Many historians have argued that the provision of mass schooling was an inevitable response to Britain's declining industrial position. That is to say, mass education was a technological necessity. On the other hand Marxist analyists argue that state schools were provided to ensure the production of an orderly and compliant workforce and to stifle the growth of working-class resistance to the forces of industrial capitalism. An examination of contemporary documents and speeches lend some support to both positions.

It is important to bear in mind that before and during this early period of elementary schooling the children of the upper and middle classes were being educated separately in their own institutions. The boys of the upper classes in the public schools, the boys of the middle classes in the endowed grammar schools. Girls from these classes were most likely to be educated at home by governesses or to be excluded from any formal education other than preparation in wifely skills. In the elementary schools also the emphasis for girls tended to be upon 'useful' domestic work, a curriculum that stressed their future position in life as poorly paid domestic servants or wives and mothers.

In 1902 the School Boards were replaced by the system of Local Education Authorities and these Authorities were empowered to establish their own secondary schools. In 1907 a free-place system made scholarships available at these state grammar schools.

Table 2.1 shows the social class composition of grammar schools in three areas around the period of the introduction of the free-place system.

For the vast majority of working-class pupils their only access to formal education was through the elementary school system. And the secondary and elementary school traditions developed quite separately.

The 1944 Education Act

In 1917 the Board of Education, which then had overall responsibility for state provision, established the Secondary Schools Examination Council in an effort to coordinate standards and curtail the influence of the university examination boards. A system of School Certificates, forerunners of today's O- and A-levels, was formalised. In effect the curriculum of the secondary schools was fixed and finalised for the next forty years as a

Table 2.1

Social class composition of Hightown Grammar School (1905–17)
compared with south-west Hertfordshire and Middlesbrough Grammar
Schools (per cent).

	S.W. Herts 1904–18	Middlesbrough 1905–18	Hightown 1905–17
Professional, managerial and owning	31·3	29·8	15·9
Retail trade, clerks, foremen	54·2	46·4	49.7
Skilled and unskilled workers	14·5	22·8	34·5
Totals	100·0	100·0	100·0
N =	873	993	760

Source: Lacey, C. *Hightown Grammar*, Manchester University Press, (1970) p.11.

result of the regulations issued by the Examinations Council in 1918. The main elements of this curriculum are still clearly in place in the contemporary comprehensive school.

This basic structure of provison remained intact until the passing the 1944 Education Act. This Act, based on the 1939 Report of the Spens Committee and the 1943 Report of the Norwood Committee, offered free secondary education for all, based upon a tripartite system of schools; three different sorts of schools for children with three different 'types of mind'. The 'secondary grammar' pupil who 'is interested in learning for its own sake'; the 'secondary technical' pupil whose interests and abilities lie markedly in the field of applied science or applied art'; and the 'secondary modern' pupil, who 'deals more easily with concrete things than with ideas. . . He (sic) is interested in things as they are; he finds little attraction in the past or in the slow disentanglement of causes or movements'. The pupils would be allocated to the appropriate school primarily on the basis of the 11+ examination, although the Norwood Report noted that 'The first classification of pupils would necessarily be tentative in a number of cases, for the diagnosis of special interests and skills demanding a curriculum suited to them takes time'. The schools were to be accorded 'parity of amenities' and 'parity of esteem', although with regard to the latter the report notes that 'parity of esteem in our view cannot be conferred by administrative decree nor by equality of cost per pupil, it can only be won by the school itself'. It was hoped and expected that the system of 11+ examining, the raising of the school-leaving age to 15 (in 1947) and the abolition of fees would ensure that social-class barriers between different types of provision would be ended. As we have seen already this was not to be the case. Middle-class pupils tended to be over-represented in the grammar schools, working-class pupils over-represented in the secondary modern schools (look again at Table 1.1). The majority of Local Authorities did not avail themselves of the possibility of establishing technical schools. The initial implementation of the 1944 Act took place during the Labour government of 1945–51, and indeed the thinking behind the tripartite system fitted quite well with the meritocratic tradition of the Labour Party. The new Ministry of Education and the Labour Minister of Education during this period discouraged the Local Authorities that wished to introduce multilateral or comprehensive schools. Nonetheless during this time, and in the 13 years of Conservative government which followed, the number of comprehensive schools began to grow. From a mere 13 in 1951 to 138 (out of 5847) in 1961. Successive Conservative Ministers of Education countenanced setting up of comprehensive schools only in areas where existing grammar schools would not be affected (e.g. in new towns).

Comprehensive schools

During this period of Conservative government there was increasing pressure within the Labour Party (in particular from the LCC (the London County Council) and the National Association of Labour Teachers (NALT) for a firm commitment to comprehensive education. But the acceptance of the new policy was slow in coming and was hedged around with continued support for grammar schools. As late as 1963 Harold Wilson, asked whether the Labour Party would abolish grammar schools, replied with the much quoted 'Over my dead body'. Nonetheless, the commitment to introduce comprehensive schools was a part of the party manifesto for the 1964 election and some commentators have argued that it swayed at least some middle-class parents, who could not get their children into grammar schools, towards a Labour vote. Clearly, the secondary modern schools were unpopular with many parents. Poor facilities and high levels of staff turnover were frequent complaints. Most teachers were non-graduates with only one or two years training and their salaries were lower than those of their grammar school counterparts. But more than anything else the secondary moderns were tainted as schools for failures. Even the successful and innovatory schools with good facilities and well-designed courses could not escape from the stamp of failure.

In 1965, the new Labour government issued Circular 10/65, and as if to underline their still wavering commitment, the circular *requested* Local Authorities to submit plans for comprehensive reorganisation. It was not for another 11 years and two governments later that the 1976 Education Act was passed requiring such reorganisation.

To be sure the majority of authorities did submit schemes, by 1969 only 22 out of almost 300 Authorities had no acceptable reorganisation plans. But many more had only partial plans or did not envisage implementation in the short term. The Conservative Party returned to power in 1970 with Margaret Thatcher as Secretary of State for Education. Circular 10/65 was rescinded and Mrs Thatcher rejected proposed changes to 326 schools in 36 LEAs submitted to her during the next four years. Nonetheless, paradoxically, the pace of reorganisation increased during this period. In 1969 26.2 per cent of all state secondary pupils were in comprehensive schools. In 1974 this had risen to 62.0 per cent, and in 1978 the figure was 83 per cent. (The practice of comprehensive schooling is discussed in the following section.) However, these overall figures tend to hide the fact that a large proportion of LEAs (25 out of 97 in 1982) still retain some form of selection. This usually takes the form of the retention of one grammar school (catering for on average five per cent of secondary pupils) within a supposedly comprehensive system. But the challenge to the principle of comprehensive education is not limited to the retention of a small number of super-selective grammar schools.

The policies of the Conservative Party, returned to power in 1979, also pose a threat to the continuation of comprehensive schooling in any meaningful sense. There are a number of examples. In 1981 the Assisted Places Scheme was introduced. This scheme provides scholarships for pupils in the state system to attend private schools. This results both in the creaming off of more able pupils from the comprehensives and pumps state monies into the private sector. Meanwhile within the comprehensives the Technical and Vocational Education Initiative (TVEI) and pilot schemes aimed at providing special courses for the 'bottom 40 per cent of ability' may have the effect of re-introducing firm lines of differentiation between pupils from the age of 14+. Following the announcement of plans for TVEI the *Times Higher Education Supplement,* anticipating many subsequent criticisms, noted that:

> The danger of Mr Tebbit's proposal is that some 14-year-olds would receive an impoverished education which left them with inadequate skills to achieve the social autonomy that is their right as citizens, and the economic adaptability that is their duty, and safeguard, as workers.
>
> *THES*, 19 November 1982.

The other significant point about the TVEI scheme is that it is financed not by the Department of Education and Science, but by the Manpower Services Commission. The schools involved in the scheme are required to sign contracts with the MSC, having had their proposals for TVEI teaching approved in advance. This injection of cash comes at a time when the normal sources of funding for schools, channelled through the LEAs, have been severely cut. LEAs and schools find it difficult to turn down the offer of additional teaching and material resources but in accepting funding directly from government they are beginning to lose some of the autonomy that has existed in the British education system over the past 50 years.

Youth unemployment

Finally, in a review of mass schooling it is important to note that one of the side effects of the recent massive increases in youth unemployment is a resulting growth in the numbers of young people staying on in some form of education beyond 16 years of age. Until fairly recently the majority of 16-year-olds went straight into some form of employment, only about 25 per cent staying on for A-level courses and a small proportion going into further education for vocational training. This pattern has changed drastically with the introduction through the MSC of the Youth Training Scheme (YTS). All school leavers are being offered a year of training and preparation for work, wholly or partly based in an employer's premises. What is happening in effect is the extension of the normal endpoint of full-time education for the majority of teenagers from 16 years to 17 or 18. Once the school based TVEI scheme is fully operational it provides a natural precursor to YTS and a separate 'stream' of education (or training) will be established. Pupils of 'higher ability' will continue with academic subjects in the new GCSE (General Certificate of Secondary Education) curriculum. A form of 'educational apartheid' will be established. There may be a great deal that is intrinsically worthwhile in schemes like TVEI and YTS but while they recruit only pupils of 'lower ability' then their general effect is likely to be socially divisive and a travesty of the concept of comprehensive education.

The comprehensive experience

Comprehensive education remains a highly contentious public issue in Britain, but one of the difficulties that arises in any discussion of it is that the concept of comprehensive education lacks any clear definition or common agreement. Despite the advent of Circular 10/65 and the 1976 Education Act the Labour governments involved failed to set out positive objectives for comprehensive schooling. Their concerns were entirely with matters of structure, a comprehensive system, rather than with practice.

Very few of the outlines and definitions which come from other sources go further than offering general educational ideals, and the vacuum created by the absence of guidelines related to practice has only tended to perpetuate the values and attitudes of selective schooling within the new comprehensives.

Examination of the literature on comprehensive education from political parties, LEAs, teacher unions, education pressure groups and educationalists generally, suggests that three different models or conceptions of comprehensive education are represented in the overall debate. These may be considered as the meritocratic, the integrative and the egalitarian.

1 *The meritocratic view* rests on the notion of 'equality of opportunity'. The idea is that everyone should start with an equal chance to succeed. Much the same thinking originally lay behind the tripartite system, but here it is associated with everyone going to the same school. Once inside the school the most academically able will be identified over time and be provided with the most appropriate courses to exploit and suit their talents. The survival of the cleverest. Other pupils will be catered for according to their talents to ensure that everyone has the opportunity to realise their full potential, but it is taken for granted that differences, not to say inequalities, will emerge over time. Such schools would typically be streamed or set, and offer a differentiated curriculum, but primarily they are concerned with the pursuit of academic goals. Little account is taken here of social inequalities that may arise from class or cultural differences originating from outside the school.

2 *The integrative view* was strongly represented in the Labour Party thinking on comprehensive education in the 1950s and 1960s. The assumption is that by providing one school for all, with social classes mixed together, greater tolerance and social harmony will result and class tensions will abate. It is not necessarily assumed that social classes will disappear but rather that they will be more tolerant of one another. Here the goals for the comprehensive school are primarily social rather than academic, schooling is to be employed as a form of social engineering, to change society. Conservative critics of the comprehensive principle have been particularly fervent in their objections to these ideas.

3 *The egalitarian view* is the most radical and pays greatest attention to changes in the process of schooling. What is stressed here is equality of outcome rather then equality of opportunity. Streaming would be abolished, a common curriculum established, and the barriers between school and the outside world reduced. Pupils would be treated as of equal worth, with greatest resources devoted to those who find school most difficult. This position is normally articulated by representatives of the political left and is identified with 'progressive education' in general. (In many respects Countesthorpe College in Leicestershire is one of the few comprehensives to have attempted seriously to organise

itself along these lines. Since opening, the school has faced a constant barrage of criticism from parents and politicians.)

The predominance of the meritocratic conception of comprehensive education is evident in my own case study of a comprehensive school (Ball, 1981) and that of Burgess (Burgess, R.G., *Experiencing Comprehensive Education,* Methuen, London, (1983). Both schools are oriented to academic education with the result that many pupils experience school as 'failures'.

The period in the 1960s during which comprehensive education appeared to have gained popular and political support (even from the Conservatives), the so-called 'progressive consensus', probably lasted for less than five years. The beginning of the end of this brief and fragile consensus can probably be associated with the publication of the first of the Black papers in 1969 (Cox, C.B. and Dyson, A.E. (eds) *The Fight for Education,* The Critical Quarterly Society) a series of trenchant attacks on the idea of comprehensive education from the political right. Since that time comprehensive schools have come under increasing criticism both from a whole range of entrenched opponents, who argue that the new system has failed to live up to the best of grammar school education, and from supporters who have been disappointed at the extent to which the new schools have been unable to shake off grammar school traditions and practices. Comprehensive reform has been throughout an ad hoc, often half-hearted process, which has been set within powerful political and economic constraints.

All of this creates particular problems when it comes to the question of researching and evaluating comprehensive schooling. One of the commonest methods for evaluation is to attempt to compare the examination performance of comprehensives with grammar schools. This strategy has two problems, one technical and one educational. Technically such comparisons are fraught with difficulties. As we have noted many comprehensives are 'creamed' by selective schools, the most able pupils are directed elsewhere. Furthermore, in the background the private system continues to attract approximately 6 per cent of secondary age pupils. The Assisted Places Scheme is adding to the creaming effect. Educationally the concentration on examination results is dubious and unfortunate, but for many commentators this is the be-all and end-all of education. (See Marks, J. Cox, C. and Pomian-Szednicki, M., *Standards in English Schools,*

National Council for Educational Standards (1983). Paradoxically, while studies of examination results continue to attract
publicity and put comprehensive schools under pressure to
perform better, the schools are also being required to take on
board a whole range of innovations – TVEI, computer literacy,
links with industry, etc. – which are actually intended to reduce
the overall emphasis on the academic aspects of schooling.
Altogether, the comprehensive experience remains both con-
troversial and confused.

3 The role and function of education – selection or social reproduction?

In this section we will examine competing explanations of the role and function of education in society. One, functionalism, is based on the assumption that social institutions and social processes can be explained by attributing to them functions which are necessary for the survival of the society. The other, Marxism, rests upon a distinction between the economic base or mode of production of a particular society – e.g. feudalism or capitalism – and it superstructure, consisting of legal, political and educational arrangements, and ethical, philosophical and political beliefs. The economic base is regarded as determining, to a greater or lesser extent, the elements of the superstructure. Further, and of major importance here, the superstructure is seen as largely serving the purpose of maintaining the conditions necessary for production. The terms functionalism and Marxism will serve us here as general labels for types of theory. In fact it is possible to identify a range of different positions and interpretations within each theoretical field, as functionalists and Marxists disagree amongst themselves as often as they disagree with one another.

Functionalism and education

The major figures normally associated with functionalism are Emile Durkheim, **Talcott Parsons** and Robert Merton. Each present a particular version of functionalism and in their prolific writings they each had a great deal to say about education. But for our purposes we will concentrate on Parsons who is specifically identified with structural-functionalism. He produced a highly abstract analysis to account for the relationship between individuals and their society. He was very much concerned with the problem of social order in society. Lockwood explains Parsons' position very clearly (see Fig. 3.1).

So as Lockwood explains, Parsons focuses his attention on the

Fig. 3.1   Parsons' structural-functionalism.

For Parsons, the social system is a system of action. It is made up of the interactions of individuals. Of special concern to sociology is the fact that such interactions are not random but mediated by common standards of evaluation. Most important among these are moral standards, which may be called norms. Such norms 'structure' action. Because individuals share the same 'definition of the situation' in terms of such norms, their behaviour can be intermeshed to produce a 'social structure'. The regularity, or patterning, of interaction is made possible through the existence of norms which control the behaviour of actors. Indeed, a stabilised social system is one in which behaviour is regulated in this way, and, as such, is a major point of reference for the sociological analysis of the dynamics of social systems. It is necessary in sociology, as in biology, to single out relatively stable points of reference, or 'structural' aspects of the system under consideration, and then to study the processes whereby such structures are maintained. This is the meaning of the 'structural-functional' approach to social system analysis. Since the social system is a system of action, and its structural aspects are the relatively stable interactions of individuals around common norms, the dynamic processes with which the sociologist is concerned are those which function to maintain social structures, or, in other words, those processes whereby individuals come to be motivated to act in conformity with normative standards.

Lockwood, D. (1956) pp.282–83.

stable structures within society and the processes which maintain and ensure the continuance of these structures. A primary element in this maintenance are those social processes which achieve the social conformity of individuals to established norms and values. Parsons' emphasis was upon the stability of society and upon consensus among the social actors who make up society. He outlines four basis functional imperatives (see Fig. 3.2) which he felt to be the basic necessities for the achievement of consensus and the continued operation of a society (or any social institution for that matter). These are the stable structures referred to above.

Fig. 3.2   The functional imperatives
The four are as follows:

Adaptation – the provision of the physical necessities of life: food, shelter, clothes, etc. This is the function of the economic system; factories, banks, agriculture.

Goal attainment – the setting of aims and objectives for social action and the determination of the means of achieving these. This is the function of the polity, the political system: government, state agencies, political parties and pressure groups.

Pattern maintenance and *tension management* – the maintenance of necessary levels of motivation among individuals and the resolution of interpersonal conflicts. This is the function of the kinship system, families and marriages. Socialisation plays an important part.

Integration – it is necessary to ensure coordination between the various aspects of society, and social control in relations between social actors. This is the function of cultural and community organisations: schools, churches and mass media. These institutions socialise their members into the social values of the society. If social control breaks down then the police and law courts may be called upon to formally uphold and reinforce basic values that are embodies in law. Here then we can easily see how the education system plays its part in the maintenance of society, at this abstract level, by socialising individuals and thus ensuring conformity to basic norms and values.

Functional imperatives and education

Two further points have to be made. First, the system of analysis by functional imperatives can be applied at any level. The same necessities identified within the social system as a whole have to be fulfilled within the cultural sub-system and within individual cultural organisations. Thus, according to Parsons it should be possible to identify the sub-systems within a school (or a classroom) which serve each of the basic functional imperatives. Second, the four sub-systems have to be understood as interrelated and interdependent. They do not operate in isolation, rather the functions and activities of each one serve the requirments of each of the others. The family prepares and maintains, so to speak, workers for the economic system. They are fed and housed, and provided with affection and comfort by their marriage partners. By producing children the family also ensures a new generation of potential workers. The education system works in a similar way. And one of the prime functions of the education system vis-a-vis the economy is the selection and socialisation of the potential workers. This operates in two ways. First, the education system inculcates certain technical skills and requirements. Some of them general, like numeracy and literacy, others more specifically job-related. Second, the system also separates out potential workers for different points of entry to the labour market – it selects them. Underlying both of these is the socialisation of the students to accept their lot as right and appropriate. Selection is of no use if it results in a frustrated and unhappy workforce who regard themselves as failures or as hard done by. They must see the system to be fair. Some of this is made clear in the following extract from Parsons' own analysis of the school class as a social system.

To conclude this discussion of the elementary school class, something should be said about the fundamental conditions underlying the process which is, as we have seen, simultaneously (1) an emancipation of the child from primary emotional attachment to his family, (2) an internalisation of a level of societal values and norms that is a step higher than those he can learn in his family alone, (3) a differentiation of the school class in terms both of actual achievement and of differential valuation of achievement, and (4) from society's point of view, a selection and allocation of its human resources relative to the adult role system. Probably the most fundamental condition underlying this process is the sharing of common values by the two adult agencies involved – the family and the school – in this case the core of the shared valuation of achievement. It includes, above all, recognition that it is fair to give differential rewards for different levels of achievement, so long as there has been fair access to opportunity, and fair that these rewards lead on to higher-order opportunities for the successful. There is thus a basic sense in which the elementary school class is an embodiment of the fundamental American value of equality of opportunity, in that it places value both on initial equality and on differential achievement.

> Parsons, T. 'The school class as a social system: Some of its functions in American society, *Harvard Educational Review,* (1959) v.29, pp.297–318.

A fair system?

It is possible to discern here some parallels with the British 'political arithmetic' tradition. There is a basic assumption that when working properly the education system is fair and efficient. This fairness ensures that it is only differences related to intelligence and ability that produce 'different levels of achievement'. It is taken for granted that other factors stemming from social class, gender and racial differences should not be allowed to interfere, although there is a recognition that the sharing of values between home and school is a fundamental condition to the education process. If the education system is 'malfunctioning' then both the fairness and efficiency of the allocation process are threatened, and wastage and injustices will result. This is exactly the point of Halsey and Floud's criticisms of the grammar school system, as we saw in the Introduction. And the identification of the possibility of mismatches between the values of the home and those of the school, especially over the importance of achievement, provided the major area for investigation of social class inequalities.

> Selection at 11+ and segregation into separate schools is evidently a form of vocational as well as educational selection and is undesirable, because premature. It is sometimes defended in the post-war conditions of full competition for grammar school places as a promoter of social mobility and as a desirable method of selecting the best brains of all classes to form a much needed democratic elite. In fact the post-war expansion of opportunity for working-class children to enter

grammar schools directs attention away from the dysfunction-
al aspects of the system which we have been describing. . .
The most radical inference is that English education should
be reorganised along comprehensive lines.

> Floud, J and Halsey A.H. 'Education and occupation:
> English secondary schools and the supply of labour',
> *The Yearbook of Education,* (1956) London, Evans, p.530.

Here **Floud and Halsey** directly link their critique of the system
of selection at 11+ to arguments in favour of the introduction of
a comprehensive system. While Floud and Halsey made no
explicit statement of their theoretical position, their use of terms
in the quotation above indicates that they were working within
an implicit structural-functionalist analysis of education.

The strengths of the structural-functionalist approach to
education lie primarily in the emphasis that it gives to interrelationships between the education system and aspects of the wider
social structure. In particular, in highlighting the links between
education and the economy, the processes of selection and
differentiation within schools and the resulting distribution of
'life chances', become issues of central concern in the sociology
of education. This leads on to further interest in the process of
social mobility and the structure of the stratification system. Also
in this complex of interrelationships the family–school link
becomes a major focus. And underpinning this is always the
fundamental issue of values and the socialising and integrating
functions of education. In many respects functionalism defined
the agenda for British sociology of education for almost 25 years
after the second world war. But increasingly during this period
functionalism was coming under criticism.

The problem of social change

Almost all the statements of criticism against functionalism
begin, quite appropriately, with the problem of social change. As
I have indicated already the basic concepts and explanatory
framework of functionalist analyses stress the continuance and
survival of the social system. Value consensus, socialisation and
integration all emphasise the maintenance of the stability of the
system at the cost of recognising or explaining processes of

social change. Closely linked to this is the point that functionalism tends to neglect and underestimate the extent of conflict
within society as a whole. Certainly in the field of education the
recognition of conflict seems indispensable. The goals and
purposes of education are not generally agreed. Conflicts over
the definition of the school arise at several levels. Between the
school's teachers and the LEA (as in the cases of Risinghill,
Summerhill Academy and William Tyndale). Among teachers
themselves over the aims and purposes of schooling and the best
means of implementing these. And between teachers and pupils.
None of these arenas of conflict can be adequately handled from
a functionalist perspective. Furthermore, functionalism with its
emphasis on selection, socialisation and technical training in
education tends to lead to a concentration of the 'inputs' and
'outputs', or end products, of the education system, its
'boundary-exchanges' with other systems. This results in the
neglect of both the 'content' of education – the curriculum – and
teacher–pupil interaction in the classroom. Finally, in its exclu-
sive reliance on objective functions and the consequences of
patterns of collective behaviour, functionalism excludes consideration of the goals, motives and interpretations of individual
actors. Indeed Parsons has been accused of operating with a
strongly 'over-socialised' conception of social actors. They are
reduced to 'cultural dopes', in effect being nothing more than
the product of the societal norms and values which they internalise through their experiences of socialisation in the home,
school, workplace, etc. Such a conception does little justice to
the complexity and diversity of human motives which can be
readily uncovered in almost any social setting.

Marxism and education: Althusser

Marx himself had little to say directly about education, although
his few asides clearly place the education system within his
general analysis of capitalist society. He certainly viewed education as involved in ideological work, with few educational
subjects being able to escape from the danger of ideological
distortion under capitalism. But recent Marxist analysis has
placed the ideological aspects of education within a broader
framework which focuses upon the necessity of the reproduction

of the conditions of production in capitalist society. That is to say, both the physical means of production, raw materials, machinery, transport, etc., must be produced and labour power must be reproduced if capitalist production is to continue. Part of this reproduction of labour power is accomplished through the simple expedient of the payment of wages, which are used to buy food, clothing and shelter. But the school system also has a vital part to play. According to **Louis Althusser** (1972), a French Marxist philosopher, the school serves to mould individuals into subjects that fit with the requirements of capitalism, they learn submission, deference and respect for the established organisation of work and their place in it. The school also works to ensure that the labour force is technically competent.

> What do children learn at school? They go varying distances in their studies, but at any rate they learn to read, to write and to add – i.e. a number of other things as well, including elements (which may be rudimentary or on the contrary thoroughgoing) of 'scientific' or 'literary culture', which are directly useful in the different jobs in production (one instruction for manual workers, another for technicians, a third for engineers, a final one for higher management etc.). Thus they learn 'know-how'. But besides these techniques and knowledges, and in learning them, children at school also learn the 'rules' of good behaviour, i.e. the attitude that should be observed by every agent in the division of labour according to the job he is 'destined' for: rules of morality, civic and professional conscience, which actually means rules of respect for the socio-technical division of labour and ultimately the rules of the order established by class domination. They also learn to 'speak proper French', to 'handle' the workers correctly, i.e. actually (for the future capitalists and their servants) to 'order them about' properly, i.e. (ideally) to 'speak to them' in the right way, etc.
>
> Althusser (1972) pp.245–246.

Also according to Althusser the ruling class within any society must exercise control over and through schooling and the other Ideological State Apparatuses (ISAs), like the church, the family, and the mass media. The role of such apparatuses is to mystify, through ideologies, the way in which people experience the world. The ideologies themselves express the material interests of the ruling class. Thus, this control over and through the ISAs maintains what is called class hegemony, or domination. On occasion the ISAs may have to be supported by other agencies of capitalism, the so-called Repressive State Apparatuses (RSAs), like the courts and judiciary, the police and military, which operate primarily through the use of violence, rather than ideology. But ideology is the main plank of Althusser's analysis. For him ideology is fundamental and pervasive in all aspects of social life, even the most trivial interchanges and rituals of daily living. In these terms the teaching process is ideological in itself, as well as disseminating ideological views about the world. Teachers are in effect agents of capitalism who through their classroom work reproduce the exploitative relations of capitalism. They produce pupil 'types' who will accordingly receive more or less education and enter the labour force at different points.

Althusser is drawing attention to the powerful effects of the 'hidden curriculum' of schooling, what schools do to pupils by way of socialisation. Pupils learn, he argues, a respect for the workings of capitalism – the importance of time, private property, loyalty, honesty and discipline. Social order is thus maintained, and good workers are produced (although many industrialists would disagree with Althusser and are very critical of the attitudes of school leavers). The ideology of schooling, that is the social learning it produces, is its key feature. Teachers transform the consciousness of their pupils and thus fulfil one of the major social requirements for the perpetuation of capitalism, its reproduction through time, that is the provision of a skilled and docile workforce.

One of the major criticisms of Althusser is that his conception of human beings, like that of functionalism, is unduly passive and deterministic. There is little room for manoeuvre either for teachers, as the agents of capitalism, or for pupils as the victims of schooling. (As we shall see, later writers have attempted to remedy this). But Althusser does at least recognise the existence of a small minority of 'hero teachers' who see through, and penetrate, the mysteries of capitalism and teach against the dominant ideology.

I ask the pardon of those teachers who, in dreadful conditions, attempt to turn the few weapons they can find in the history and learning they 'teach' against the ideology, the system and the practices in which they are trapped. They are a kind of hero. But they are rare and how many (the majority) do not even begin to suspect the 'work' the system (which is bigger than they are and crushes them) forces them to do, or worse, put all their heart and ingenuity into performing it with the most advanced awareness (the famous new methods!).

Althusser (1972) p.261.

Social stratification of pupils

To a great extent Althusser's analysis remains abstract. He does little to ground his account of the educational process in the lived realities of the classroom. But other writers have brought Marxism to bear upon the most immediate aspects of teacher–pupil interaction. **Sharp and Green** (1975), for example, in their participant observation study of a 'progressive' primary school suggest that the teachers' organisation of classroom activities produce a differentiation between distinct 'types' of pupils. This typing then provides the basis for a social stratification of pupils within the classroom. The types emerge in part from the teachers' degree of understanding of different pupils and their problems and in part from the teachers' solutions for the practical problems of classroom management.

Sharp and Green identify three pupil types. First, there are the 'ideal' pupils, the bright, easily controlled minority, who are self-motivated and need little of the teacher's time and attention, they can 'get on' on their own. These pupils are easily understood and identified with, their behaviour and their few learning problems 'make sense' to the teacher. Second, there are the majority of 'normal' pupils. These take up most of the teacher's time but again their problems are not difficult to understand or to deal with. With help they can be kept busy and do not require a lot of thinking about. Third, there are the few 'problem' children, these are often regarded as 'peculiar' or disturbed. In normal circumstances they are incapable of getting on alone, of being 'busy'. They require a great deal of time and attention, without which they begin to create behaviour difficulties. They are not easily understood by their teachers either intellectually or morally. One strategy for coping with these pupils, which Sharp and Green observed, involved removing them from the mainstream of classroom activities and allowing them to spend time playing in the Wendy House. This was justified in terms of enabling the pupils to 'play out' their problems. They were adjudged not to be 'ready' for normal classroom work. In this way they ceased to be a continual drain on the teacher's scarce supply of time and attention.

The paradox here is that the differentiation of pupils and the school stratification it gives rise to are products of a child-centred ethos which rejects the idea of a fixed hierarchy of pupil identities. But what Sharp and Green are suggesting 'is that hierarchisation, and the differentiation of the material life chances of the children is being produced within the social structure of the classroom' (p.124). Here Sharp and Green attempt to link classrom practice at the micro level with the reproduction of class relations within society generally. Furthermore, they stress continually that the processes of differentiation they identify emerge out of the field of constraints within which the teacher's work is set. In the classroom, given these constraints, only certain solutions and ways of coping are possible.

Reproduction theory and the correspondence principle: Bowles and Gintis

The writers who are most closely identified with what has come to be known as reproduction theory are the Americans **Bowles and Gintis**. Their major work, *Schooling in Capitalist America*, published in 1976, presents a rebuttal of what they call 'liberal ideology' in educational theory. In particular, they reject the notion that mass schooling in capitalist society provides for socio-economic equality and enables the fulfilment of individual talent and potential. On the contrary they aim to demonstrate that school achievement and pupils' life chances are determined to a great extent by family background, and that the pupils' experience of schooling is essentially alienating in ways that are closely parallel to the alienation produced by work in capitalist societies. Marx had argued that workers experienced alienation as a result of being involved in a process where the product of their labour belonged to someone else. Work does not satisfy the needs of the worker, they are not in charge of their own labour

Fig. 3.3   The correspondence principle
The educational system helps integrate youth into the economic system, we believe, through a structural correspondence between its social relations and those of production. The structure of social relations in education not only inures the student to the discipline of the workplace, but develops the types of personal demeanour, modes of self-presentation, self-image, and social-class identifications which are crucial ingredients of job adequacy. Specifically, the social relationships of education – the relationships between administrators and teachers, teachers and students, students and students, and students and their work – replicate the hierarchical division of labour. Hierarchical relations are reflected in the vertical authority lines from administrators to teachers to students. Alienated labour is reflected in the student's lack of control over his or her education, the alienation of the student from the curriculum content, and the motivation of school work through a system of grades and other external rewards rather than the student's integration with either the process (learning) or the outcome (knowledge) of the educational 'production process'. Fragmentation in work is reflected in the institutionalised and often destructive competition among students through continual and ostensibly meritocratic ranking and evaluation. By attuning young people to a set of social relationships similar to those of the workplace, schooling attempts to gear the development of personal needs to its requirements.

Bowles, S. and Gintis, H. *Schooling in Capitalist America*, London, Routledge and Kegan Paul, (1976) pp.131–21.

and they are paid as little as possible so as to maximise the profits of the capitalist owner. Bowles and Gintis see schooling as operating in a similar way. Unlike other critics of the school they are not simply saying that the school has somehow failed. Rather, their point is that schooling takes the form it does in order to effectively prepare pupils for their future roles as workers under capitalism (see Fig. 3.3). This preparation is achieved primarily through the correspondence in structure, processes and social relations between the school and the workplace.

School and workplace

In general terms then the form of schooling under capitalism embodies this correspondence. A correspondence between the institution of the school and the workplace. But beyond this Bowles and Gintis argue that the experience of schooling differs according to level, and that these differences are related to the particular point of entry into the labour force for which they prepare. The internal organisation of the school will correspond with the particular point in the division of labour that its graduates are destined for. Thus, for the lowest positions of employment in industry 'rule-following' is the predominant concern. In the middle positions 'dependability' is of greatest importance, together with the ability to work independently without immediate supervison. In the senior positions the emphasis is upon the internalisation of the norms of the business, in other words they must believe in what they are doing. These differences may be seen both in time and in grouping allocations. The longer the students stay on the more likely they are to accept the norms of the institution as valid and worthwhile and become able to work on their own without teacher supervision. If pupils are grouped by ability for teaching purposes, streamed or set, then it is usually those of lower ability, the bottom stream, who are most closely supervised. They are regarded as 'unable to "get on" on their own'.

These variations in social relationships and social structure are in turn, Bowles and Gintis argue, related to the social class backgrounds of the pupils. As we have seen already, working-class students are less likely to stay on at school than their middle-class counterparts. Pupils from racial and ethnic minorities will also find themselves 'concentrated in schools whose repressive, arbitrary, generally chaotic internal order, coercive authority structures and minimal possibilities for advancement mirror the characteristics of inferior job situations' (Bowles and Gintis, p 132). Bowles and Gintis present both historical and statistical data to support their basic position, that the social background of pupils' is the primary determinant of their attainment at school (in terms of years of completed education) rather than their cognitive ability (in terms of intelligence test scores). While schooling is normally presented as being meritocratic, Bowles and Gintis see this as ideology, obscuring the real situation, where it is social background that ultimately determines occupational attainment. The workings of the school system are tied to and reflect the workings of capitalism. Educational reforms can do little to change the basic functionings of the system. Schools are efficient, but efficient in terms of the needs of capitalism.

Education and ideology

There are many broad similarities between Bowles and Gintis' work and that of Althusser. Both are concerned with the question of reproduction, the perpetuation of the social and economic requirements of capitalism, and both see the education system as shrouded in liberal ideologies about equality of opportunity, although Bowles and Gintis' conception of ideology is much narrower and more straightforward. They restrict their use of the term to sets of beliefs about the nature of social reality. Also they employ the Marxist notion of alienation, which is rejected by Althusser, who takes a purely structural position. That is to say, for Bowles and Gintis the experience of schooling is coercive and unsatisfying. Pupils work to pass examinations and satisfy the demands of their teachers rather than to satisfy their own needs for learning and understanding. As with the worker in the production process, the product of their labour is not their own. Pupils have no control over their education and their essential humanity remains unrealised. But Althusser does not accept Marx's concept of alienation and limits his analysis to the effects brought about by the economic mode of production, the demands of capitalism. Furthermore, where Bowles and Gintis limit themselves primarily to the form and processes of schooling Althusser is more aware of the content, the 'know how' that is taught in school. Althusser also takes less account of the role of the family, concentrating almost exclusively on the school.

Critics of Bowles and Gintis, and Althusser have pointed to the similarities between their arguments and the sort of analysis of the school system offered by functionalists. Indeed Althusser has been described as a functionalist Marxist. There is little room in their analyses for exceptions, for cases which do not fit. Both positions have been taken to task for their failure to take account of the occurrence of working–class resistance to the capitalist order, and as a result difficulties arise in explaining social change. Ultimately, of course, they see social change as dependent upon economic and political change.

Finally, in this section I want to give a brief account of some more recent work by neo–Marxist researchers. In one sense this will involve moving away from direct consideration of the role and function of education. However, in each case the material presented complements the Marxist position outlined above.

Learning to labour

Paul Willis' (1977) study *Learning to Labour*, was without doubt one of the most influential publications in the sociology of education during the 1970s. Indeed its impact has spread well beyond the boundaries of the sociology of education. Willis' study of a group of recalcitrant working–class pupils, 'the lads', in a Midlands comprehensive employed ethnographic research methods, i.e. participant observation and interviewing (see Fig. 3.4). It attempts to capture and present the experiences of 'the lads' at school and their attitudes and feelings towards school.

The clarity and eloquence of Willis' argument does much to strengthen his case, and 'the lads' emerge vividly in living form from the printed page. The combination of ethnography and Marxist analysis also achieves a version of synthesis between the macro and the micro. And the analysis itself marks a distinct move away from the mechanistic 'social reproduction' theories of Althusser, and Bowles and Gintis. 'The lads' are not unwitting and passive 'subjects' of processes that they fail to recognise or engage with. Their 'resistance' adds a whole new dimension to the understanding of school life and has been taken up vigorously by other writers. But as ever there are important criticisms: the adequacy of the sample of 12 'lads' has been questioned, the resistance of 'the lads' may by untypical; the lack of attention to the conformist pupils the so called 'ear oles' also creates problems, as does Willis' unquestioning acceptance of 'the lads' view of the 'ear oles'; the separation of the ethnography from the

Fig. 3.4.   Paul Willis' 'lads'

In simple terms 'the lads' are anti-school, they resent and reject it. They see the mental labour of schoolwork as pointless and unmanly. They set against the values of their teachers their own powerful working-class culture. They celebrate their masculinity – money, violence, sexism and racism being at the heart of their alternative to schooling.

They are out to have 'a laff', to turn school into an area for their own activities. In Willis' terms they are resisters, they are unwilling to submit themselves to schooling and indeed they recognise only too clearly that it holds little possibility for them. In this sense they 'penetrate', that is see through, the con trick that lies at the heart of schooling, the liberal ideology of meritocracy does not fool them. Their vision of the future is to take their place alongside their fathers on the factory shop floor. Indeed much of their behaviour and their resistance is an anticipation of the shop-floor culture. But the irony in Willis' analysis is that in their resistance to school they effectively condemn themselves to working-class futures. They connive with capitalism to do its work of social reproduction. Their 'penetrations' are 'partial', they are demystifications but as Willis' explains 'the capacity for cultural penetrations has, in its real social form, resulted in a deeper and more entangled entrapment within the capitalist order' (p.123). Thus, it becomes possible 'for an unfree condition to be entered freely' (p.120).

analysis also receives frequent comment. Are the two adequately linked? There are few attempts to employ the sorts of internal checks and tests that participant observers often use in their work.) Finally, Willis has been taken to task by feminists for failing to develop an adequate analysis of patriarchy, the 'lads' sexism is only superficially explored.

The curriculum and access to knowledge

The other area where recent Marxist analysis has produced

significant developments and insights is the study of the school curriculum. In particular, Anyon (Anyon, J. (1979) and Apple (Apple, M. *Ideology and the Curriculum,* London, Routledge and Kegan Paul), (1979) have addressed themselves to the ideological aspects of school knowledge. Anyon's work on American school textbooks puts forward the argument that these texts present accounts of history and social structure which reflect the interests of certain politically and economically dominant groups. She suggests that the choice of material, the degree of emphasis given to certain events and the explanations of events can all affect the political perspective of the reader.

> The school curriculum has contributed to the formation of attitudes that make it easier for powerful groups, those whose knowlege is legitimised by school studies, to manage and control society. Textbooks not only express the dominant groups' ideologies, but also help to form attitudes in support of their social position. Indeed, the importance of ideology to the power of dominant groups increases as the use of overt social coercion declines. In the twentieth century, the authority of tradition and the legitimacy of visible methods of control, such as force, have diminished. Government and other powerful groups increasingly justify their activities by appeals to 'reason', to the logic of evidence, and to the consent of populations; the public is ostensibly called upon to make intelligent social choices.
>
> Anyon, J. (1977) p.382.

What Anyon is emphasising here is the contribution that ideology makes to overall social control. Ideology is a form of 'invisible policing' which ensures that pupils internalise the views and interests of the capitalist class. This 'policing' is achieved via the curriculum – textbooks, materials, and ideas employed in school reflect the interests and interpretations of dominant groups. The curriculum is presented as politically neutral, but this only adds to its effectiveness and ensures that alternative interpretations can be excluded on the grounds of political bias.

Apple is also particularly interested in the ways in which social and economic control occurs in schools. Not only in the ways we have already explored, through forms of discipline and the teaching of dispositions through the hidden curriculum (that is the social learning that goes on implicitly through schooling –

e.g. norms of work, obedience, and punctuality) but also through the 'forms of meaning' that school distributes. That is through the formal body of school knowledge. School knowledge is normally taken to be neutral, both in terms of what is selected for inclusion and how this content is presented. This assumption of neutrality may itself be regarded as ideological. Knowledge is presented as though it were indisputable and agreed. 'Students in most schools and in urban centres in particular are presented with a view that serves to legitimate the existing social order since change, conflict, and men and women as creators as well as receivers of values and institutions are systematically neglected' (p.102). Schools are, according to Apple, agents of selective tradition and cultural 'incorporation', they also reproduce an unequal distribution of curricular knowledge. Inequities in cultural distribution are in turn related to inequalities in social and economic power and potency. In other words schools act to distribute both popular and elite culture, cultural as well as social reproduction. Here again are the three major themes that run through recent Marxist analyses of the role and function of education. First, that schools are involved in a process of selection and allocation. This process embodies the reproduction of the existing relations of production. Second, the process itself is legitimated and hidden by an ideology of equality of opportunity. Third, both the form of schooling and the ideologically determined body of school knowledge play their part in maintaining social control and social acquiescence.

4 Sources of educational inequality: home and school

As I have indicated already, during most of the 1950s and 1960s research work in the sociology of education was dominated by the search for the answer to one question: 'How can we explain the consistent tendency for children from working-class homes to perform less well in school than their middle-class colleagues, even when they are of similar ability?' An enormous range of types of study can be considered in relation to this broad area of concern. And it would be a mistake to ignore this diversity. There are a number of ways of classifying these studies. The framework presented here is just one possibility. The material is organised and presented in five sub-sections: (a) The material environment, (b) Parental attitudes, (c) Child-rearing studies, (d) Culture and community, (e) Linguistic development and social learning. The sequence is in general terms a chronological one, which, using a few key texts, illustrates the conceptual development in this particular area of theory and research.

The material environment

Olive Banks makes the point that in the period before the Second World War the material condition of working-class life provided an obvious focus for research into differential patterns of educational achievement. The effects of poverty in terms of poor housing, poor health and malnutrition were bound to have direct and indirect effects upon a child's ability to learn at school. After the Second World War changes in living standards and the development of school welfare facilities 'led researchers to doubt whether it is any longer possible to think of poverty as the only, or indeed the major factor, in working-class underachievement.' And indeed a number of studies conducted after 1945 appeared to confirm the inadequacy of material factors as an independent basis for explaining the differences in performance between the social classes. Floud, Halsey and Martin's 1956 research into the

11+ examination in Hertfordshire and Middlesborough (Floud, J. G., Halsey, A. H. and Martin, F.M. *Social Class and Educational Opportunity,* London, Heinemann, 1956) found material differences to be of minor importance in Hertfordshire when compared with family size and the attitudes and aspirations of parents. In Middlesborough income and housing conditions did seem to play a part in distinguishing successful from unsuccessful pupils. Douglas *et al.*'s 1964 study, which reported on the primary school careers of 5,362 children born in March 1946, also found marginal effects stemming from unfavourable home conditions for children from all social classes. But while the middle-class pupils seemed to overcome such difficulties over time the working-class pupils tended to fall further behind. The implication again being that other factors were at work to differentiate the working-class home from the middle-class home.

Two major reports on educational provision conducted during this period also attempted to identify the effects of poverty on educational attainment. The Crowther Report (*15–18,* Central Advisory Council for Education, London, HMSO) 1959, and the Plowden Report (*Children and their Primary Schools,* Central Advisory Council for Education, London, HMSO) 1967 both seemed to indicate that it was only at the lowest levels of poverty and deprivation that material circumstances directly and clearly affected school performance. The overall conclusion of the Plowden study is unequivocal: 'Educational deprivation is not mainly the effect of poverty; parental attitude and maternal care are more important than the level of material needs.' (*The Plowden Report* p. 369.)

Parental attitudes

For many researchers the key to explaining social class differences in school performance lay in an appreciation of the effects on pupils of the values, attitudes and aspirations of their parents. A flood of British and American studies have sought to demonstrate that in general terms the value orientations of working-class parents tend to handicap their children in the competition for academic success at school. Concomitantly the success of some working-class pupils could be explained in terms of the similarity of the attitudes and aspirations of their parents to those of middle-class families. For example, Douglas, *et al.* identify 'parental interest' as the crucial factors. 'High interest is closely linked to high attainment, good results in the 'O' level examination and a long school life in the next generation, whereas low interest is associated with poor performance and early leaving.'

In a similar study Kahl ('Some Measurements of Academic Orientation', *American Journal of Sociology*, 70, 6, pp.669–81) (1965) attempted to explain differences in educational aspiration in a small matched sample of American schoolboys. They came from similar homes and had similar abilities, but half aspired to go to college and half did not. The difference in aspiration could be pinned down to one factor according to Kahl; 'parental pressure'. Those boys whose parents believed in 'getting ahead' and who internalised this concern tended to be sufficiently motivated to overcome the obstacles to educational progress that they met at school. Other boys whose parents 'accepted the scheme of things and their own place in it' tended not to encourage a future orientation in their children and allowed their sons to 'do as they liked'. Several of the 'getting ahead' parents seemed to be very conscious of their own failures at school and were anxious to have their sons take a serious attitude to their school work and their future education. However, some boys in the sample were not like their parents. They had not internalised their parents view of things. It is not possible to simply read off the values and aspirations of children from those of their parents and it is extremely difficult to sustain a mono-causal account of the relationship between home and school as Kahl attempts to do.

It is all too easy to accept the overall tendency of findings emerging from this kind of research and to neglect the anomalies and counter-factual evidence. Banks (1971) points out a number of problems in the home and school research. First, a number of studies have indicated the importance of recognising the existence of relative rather than absolute conceptions of ambition or mobility. That is to say, when aspirations are compared it is necessary to take account of relative baselines. The apparently modest educational or occupational aspirations of working-class pupils may still require long-range social mobility. The daughter of an unskilled labourer who intends to become a secretary may have 'higher' aspirations than the son of a bank clerk who aims to be a solicitor.

Second, the modest aspirations of working-class pupils may,

in part at least, be the result of 'realistic' adjustment to their circumstances. Aspirations are lowered and behaviour modified to fit in with immediate possibilities. This can be seen to occur in relation to both school and stream allocation. Thus, Himmelweit, Halsey and Oppenheim (The views of some adolescents on the social class structure, *British Journal of Sociology*, 1952, 3, 2 pp.148–72) found that middle-class boys in secondary modern schools expected to enter jobs of lower social prestige than did working-class boys in grammar schools.

Third, a large number of the home and school studies which focus on value differences between social classes fail to identify the actual mechanisms which link values to achievement. Statistical relationships are often small and rely upon the use of multiple indices of 'value orientation' or aspiration. It is one thing to establish that middle-class and working-class parents have different value orientations. It is much more difficult to relate these orientations directly to differences in school achievement. We have already noted Kahl's research and the existence of exceptions to the general pattern. Other studies have produced conflicting evidence. Altogether the results are far from conclusive.

Child-rearing studies

One way in which the 'theoretical and empirical gap between parental values and the school performance of the child' can be filled is to concentrate on the influence of patterns of child-rearing. What kinds of attitudes and behaviour of parents affect or influence the attitudes and behaviour of children? **Newson, Newson and Barnes** make the point that 'The classless society in Britain is still a long way off. Men (sic) may be born equal; but, within its first month in the world, the baby will be adapting to a climate of experience that varies according to its family's social class.' Again the basic argument is that the socialisation experiences of working-class children and middle-class children are distinct and the experiences of middle-class children are likely to be a better preparation for school success.

Musgrove provides a brief summary of some of the factors involved:

The 'Good home' is an aid to success in our school system. It is small; the parents are ambitious for their children; the father is at least a skilled manual worker; and if it is a working-class home, the mother has preferably 'married down'. The father is somewhat ineffectual, perhaps rather feckless; but one of both parents are demanding, even ruthless in their expectations of achievement. Relationships in the home are emotionally bleak. The family is unstable and has moved often; the mother goes to work. The children grow up to be rather withdrawn and solitary, conscientious and given to self-blame. They are 'good grammar school material'.

> Musgrove, F. *The Family, Education and Society*, London, Routledge and Kegan Paul, (1966) p.72.

Despite a considerable body of evidence of social class differences along the lines summarised by Musgrove (there are also variations within social class groups) the problem of linking these differences in behaviour with actual differences in school performance remains. Two American studies illustrate the problems. Drews and Teachan (Drews, E. and Teachan, J. 'Parental Attitudes and Academic Achievements, *Journal of Clinical Psychology*, (1957) 13, 4 pp.328–32) used questionnaires directed to mothers of under- and over-achievers at school. It was found that the mothers of high-achievers reported themselves to be more authoritarian and restrictive than the mothers of low-achievers. Morrow and Wilson (Morrow, W. and Wilson, R. 'Family Relations of Bright High-Achieving and Under-Achieving High School Boys' *Child Development*. (1961) 32, pp 501–510) collected the perceptions of their families from groups of over- and under-achieving boys and found the reverse relationship.

One more recent attempt to examine how the 'quality' of socialisation in the home affects school attainment is the work of Newson, Newson and Barnes. Their longitudinal study is based upon regular interviews with 700 mothers. They uncovered social-class differences in relation to patterns of general cultural interests (which consists of a variety of items such as whether extra lessons are paid for by parents, family visits to museums, the cinema, the zoo, etc.) and what they call 'home-school concordance' (whether the child takes things to school to show teacher, whether parents help with school work, and whether the child follows up schoolwork with parents). Clearly, these aspects of family life and parent-child interaction are more concretely related to school and achievement. The general pattern of findings is summarised as follows: As one moves from professional social groups towards unskilled manual groups, a number of changes are evident:

1 the range of cultural interests experienced by children as members of their family group becomes narrower and more restricted.

2 although children in all classes sometimes carry over school activities into the home, further down the scale they are less inquiring at home on school inspired topics.

3 parents become less inclined to take up and expand children's questions.

4 parents are, in particular, less likely to use books or newspapers to further the child's knowledge, and are more likely to attempt to conceal their own ignorance.

5 children are less likely to receive help, either direct or in the form of the encouragement of a 'hospitable environment' with schoolwork other than reading.

Newson, J. and E., and Barnes, P. *Perspectives on School at Seven Years Old,* London, Allen and Unwin, (1977).

Interestingly the study found that girls were more likely than boys to involve their parents in school related activities, the least well-off group of all being the sons of low income, unskilled manual workers. Here then is an attempt to explore the interface between school and home as a social dynamic, identifying family practices that directly advantage or disadvantage the child.

Culture and community

The interplay between the influences of the culture of the home, the community and the school is nowhere better illustrated than in **Jackson and Marsden's** classic study of 88 working-class boys and girls in Huddersfield in the late 1940s and early 1950s. The point of the study was to identify successful working-class pupils who had got to grammar school and stayed on until 18 years of age. The question then was what distinguished these pupils from others who did not succeed at school.

The majority came from relatively prosperous home-owning working-class families. Often the families could be described as 'sunken middle-class', where parents or grandparents had been downwardly mobile as a result of ill-health, bankruptcy or other misfortune. Typically they came from districts of mixed social class and an 'important minority' of middle-class children attended their primary school. But entry to the grammar school was nonetheless marked by uncertainty and confusion. They were now in a predominantly middle-class environment. The patterns of speech were different, and the other pupils were full of confidence and often better prepared by their previous schools. If they were to survive they had to adapt socially and culturally. This adaptation often created tensions between school and neighbourhood which had to be faced day by day. One girl is quoted describing the humiliation she faced when carrying her violin home through the jibes and insults of her neighbours. Parents were supportive, encouraging and eager for their children to succeed but their resources were limited. Their knowledge of the education system was often patchy and their relationships with the teacher awkward.

> The parents were on the whole peculiarly anxious that their children do well at grammar school, and we have seen too how worried and full of problems some of them already were. And yet there was this failure to take advantage of the teacher-parent relationship. Only very rarely could this be put down as simple neglect. We asked the parents why they did not go to school more, and their answers were so various, and sometimes so barely sensible, as to be merely sketchy rationalisations. Some said they were always working late or the bus journey was a difficult one – despite the fact that their children had managed it daily since the age of eleven. Others felt their attendance would upset the child, others still reported how uncomfortable they felt in the presence of the teachers and other parents. Some felt that one visit a year was worse than no use at all, and complained of the hurry and the big crowds on that night. Others again spoke of the teachers as not being interested in them or their children.
>
> Jackson, B. and Marsden, D. *Education and the Working Class*, Harmondsworth, Penguin, (1962) p.134.

These successful families were untypical of the working-class but neither were they 'of' the middle–class. Their children often found success to be tinged with pain and estrangement.

Having finished secondary school thirteen of the pupils left for jobs in accountancy, the civil service, the Forces, pharmacy or laboratories. The rest went on to college or university. Family ties were broken and not replaced. They were socially mobile but culturally rootless.

Linguistic development and social learning

Another writer whose work brings together school performance and family socialisation practices is **Basil Bernstein**. Bernstein's work on language and social class has been a major influence both within the sociology of education and upon teachers and teacher trainers. He argues that the form of socialisation in the family, particularly the form of the social relationship between parents and children, affects the development of speech. He is interested in the social antecedents of 'educability'.

Language codes and social control

Bernstein's argument is that there are certain sociological factors critical to the process of socialisation, like the parents' occupations, and the family's community or neighbourhood, which affect linguistic performance and forms of talk within the family. These forms of talk, or speech codes as Bernstein refers to them, are crucial in controlling the passing on of norms and values and creating specific social identities for family members. That is, the speech codes, the type of talk in the family, are vehicles for the perpetuation of the family culture from one generation, the parents, to the next, the children. Furthermore, the attitudes to learning, the aspirations and motivations and the forms of social control provided by the speech codes may be more or less relevent to those qualities and types of behaviour expected of pupils in school. If there is a mismatch between the home and the school the child's chances of school success are considerably reduced.

A restricted code orients the speaker to relatively context-bound speech and particularistic 'orders of meaning'. This may mean that effective communications are limited to those with whom the speaker shares many assumptions and meanings, and the speaker has problems in verbalising personal intent. Speech is also more predictable, and sentences will be shorter and less grammatical. This type of linguistic performance is associated, according to Bernstein, with position-oriented families, which are based upon prescribed family roles (mother, father, daughter, etc.). Here decision-making is vested in the highest status ranking member. The child takes over and responds to a formal pattern of obligations and privileges. The structure of communication is closed, and social control is through the imperative mode ('Stop it'. 'Because I said so'.). The child may lack autonomy but attain a strong sense of social identity.

An elaborated code orients the speaker to language use that is context-free. The speaker is not confined to the immediate and the known. Universalistic 'orders of meaning' are accessible. Principles are made explicit and are open to change as a result. This type of linguistic performance is associated with person-oriented families, which are identified with certain sections of the middle class and the more mobile and affluent sections of the working class. Here the family roles are not fixed to traditional role patterns. The parent will take account of the specific attributes of the individual child. The communication structure is differently focused, more open and more fluid than in the position-oriented family. The child is required to be more flexible and responsive to the explicit concerns and motives of others. Social control is achieved through the exploration of intentions and reasons via negotiation. Social arrangements are not taken for granted. The sequence of Bernstein's argument can be represented in diagrammatic form. (See Fig. 4.1.)

The sequence begins at the level of social structure and the differentiation and hierarchy of social classes created by a capitalist economy. This differentiation and hierarchy has influence upon the work roles of the family members and deeply penetrates the structure of life experiences within the family. These factors generate a particular form of social relation and control within the family and thence a particular form of communication. In its turn the form of communication or linguistic code that is generated will shape the affective, social and intellectual orientations of the children in a particular way. As Bernstein says, 'The social structure becomes the child's psychological reality through the shaping of his (sic) acts of

Fig. 4.1

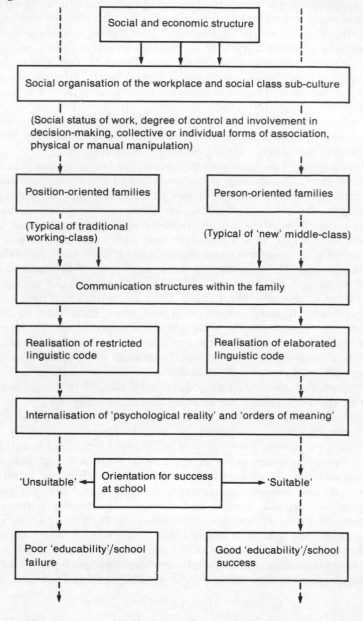

speech.' Finally, the linguistic codes are related to the likelihood of academic success in school, the child's 'educability'.

Bernstein sees the school as an institution based on the elaborated code, employing pre-eminently universalistic orders of meaning. To be successful the child requires to have access to such orders of meaning, and many working-class pupils do not. (One of the important questions is whether this is an accurate view of the nature of language use in the instruction contexts of schooling (See Cooper 1976).

Bernstein is clearly not happy with an argument which simply links the working-class unproblematically with the restricted code and the middle-class with the elaborated code. He is discussing social class here in terms of tendencies. He does not treat general class categories as homogenous. Social structure is related to school via forms of work experience and types of family. In this way the scope of Bernstein's theory is comprehensive but it is also subtle. But is it a theory? There is little empirical support for this account of variations in school achievement. In some senses Bernstein's work fits, like the rest of the material presented in this section, into the 'political arithmetic' tradition. His early papers are very much concerned with linking home and school via social class and his work has been profoundly influenced by Durkheim. But it would be dangerous to say that Bernstein's work is in any way functionalist, and his later papers bring him closer to the more radical structuralism discussed in the previous chapter. He has certainly also been influenced by the writings of Pierre Bourdieu, a French Marxist anthropologist, whose work is discussed below.

Cultural deprivation

Bernstein's work, despite his own protests, played its part, with studies on child-rearing and parental attitudes and expectations, in establishing an image of working-class family life as essentially 'culturally deprived'. That is, as lacking the cultural resources, support and stimulation which together prepare a child to take full advantage of educational experiences at school. Research on cultural differences between working-class and middle-class families appeared to produce a complete 'social pathology' of typical working-class life which powerfully explained the poor performance of many working-class children at school.

This 'deficit' view of the working-class family certainly convinced many education policy-makers and teachers. In the 1960s in Britain and the USA massive schemes of 'compensatory education' were proposed and initiated, schemes which were intended to compensate for the cultural deprivation of working-class children and improve their long term chances of educational success. In America, the best known scheme was 'Operation Headstart', a pre-school programme of play, activities and stimulation. In Britain, the programme of Educational Priority Areas, involving the provision of additional resources to schools in deprived areas is the most notable of various attempts at educational compensation. As critics have pointed out the danger of notions like 'cultural deprivation' is that they confuse deprivation with difference and can lead to the dismissal of a whole way of life. Working-class culture is assumed to be inferior and inadequate because it differs from middle-class culture. This is supported by a 'vacuum ideology', a view that there is nothing of any cultural worth in working-class life, that is, that it is culturally empty. Also, a number of writers, including Bernstein, have argued that the emphasis on 'cultural deprivation' draws attention away from economic deprivation and structural inequalities.

Cultural capital: Bourdieu

Bourdieu is one of the few Marxist sociologists of education to take seriously the relationship between home and school. He is interested in the role of schools in transferring social and cultural inequalities from one generation to the next. And he employs two crucial concepts in his account of this process of reproduction: 'habitus' and 'cultural capital'.

The habitus is essentially the culture of a particular social group or class that provides the basis for the 'durable dispostion' – the ways of seeing and making sense of the world – of the child. The habitus is constructed afresh in each generation through the children's experience of socialisation within their social group and in relation to the objective material conditions of their social world. Habitus then is the way in which a culture is embodied in an individual. The important point that follows from this is that certain habituses constitute cultural capital in relation to the processes of schooling, while others do not. This involves a combination of knowledge, intellectual style, demeanour, behaviour and language. Willis' 'lads' would be debarred on all counts.

There is an intended parallel between the idea of cultural capital and that of economic capital. The latter provides financial advantage when invested wisely, the former can provide educational advantage, and thus also, eventually, financial advantage, when invested in schooling. Bourdieu has identified the strategic use of education, as an alternative to financial investment, as a means used by certain social groups to ensure the maintenance of family status and economic position from generation to generation. The school accepts and takes for granted the cultural capital of the dominant social groups within society and proceeds as though it were equally distributed among all students. The subordinate groups, the working class, do not have cultural capital. They fail at school and thus the social hierarchies within society are perpetuated and reproduced.

In Bourdieu's terms failure is a process, a gradual 'cooling out' of the working-class pupils involving 'learned ignorance'. That is to say, schools only reward those students who accept and respond to the authority of the school and its teachers and the criteria they work with. Those working-class pupils who do not succeed must assimilate themselves and acquire the necessary cultural capital, perhaps in the ways described by Jackson and Marsden. In doing so they cease to be working class.

Education is for Bourdieu a form of cultural practice. It is also an aspect of 'symbolic violence' in society, the oppression of the working classes by cultural domination, rather than by the use of physical coercion. His argument does not rely on a view of the working-class child as culturally deprived or deficient. Indeed his analysis leads in the opposite direction towards an understanding of who controls and defines the process of schooling, as well as pointing to the need for studies of the transmission of habituses within family groups.

Contributions to the study of the process of schooling are considered in the next chapter.

5 Sources of educational inequality: inside the school

The main emphasis of 'home and school' research lay in attempts to identify the origins or causes of working-class failure in school. In most cases this failure was traced to certain 'inadequacies' of the working-class home. For the most part the school end of the relationship remained unexamined. But there were exceptions to this general pattern. During the 1960s a number of studies began to attend to the role played by streaming in schools in reinforcing and exaggerating social-class differences in attainment.

Douglas *et al's* **Medical Research Council study** *The Home and the School* provided one of the earliest and clearest statements of the critical effects of grouping pupils into streams in primary school, and the relationship of streaming to social-class differentiation. Drawing on a special study of 491 children from the 1948 sample who were in two-stream primary schools, Douglas examined changes in test score performance over a three-year period and compared the allocation to streams of children of similar abilities from different social-class backgrounds. He concluded that: 'Once allocated, the children tend to take on the characteristics expected of them and the forecasts of ability made at the point of streaming are to this extent self-fulfilling' (p.147).

At each level of ability, measured by test scores, the children in upper streams improved their scores while the scores of those in lower streams deteriorated. Furthermore, when children with the same level of measured ability were compared, 'middle-class children tended to be allocated to the upper streams and the manual working-class children to the lower ones' (p.148). Douglas goes on to suggest that this 'misallocation' is a product of the 'unconscious biases' operated by teachers in the judgements they make about pupils' abilities and that 'in the early years at primary school it seems that judgements of ability are influenced by the types of home' (p.147).

Another primary school study, **Jackson's** *Streaming: an education system in miniature* (1964), extended many of the points raised in

Douglas's work. In one part of his study Jackson surveyed 660 primary schools and found that:

> When analysed by social background, it was clear that stream-
> ing worked as a major form of social as well as academic
> selection. There were only 5 chances in 100 of a professional's
> or manger's child going into a 'D' class. It also partly divided
> children according to their date of birth. 'D' streams had twice
> as many summer-born as winter-born children. All this re-
> mained true whether streaming took place early or later, and
> whatever tests the school used didn't affect the kind of
> children who became 'A', 'B' or 'C'. (p.29)

Jackson also presents a case-study of one streamed primary school, referred to as Honey Bell. The detailed comparison of children in the A, B and C streams at Honey Bell clearly anticipates some aspects of Lacey and Hargreaves' work, which are discussed below. In particular, the patterns of friendship, separation and social–class differentiation which were found in the secondary school studies are already beginning to emerge in the primary school.

> The children saw them too. In the staff's view the children
> were 'realists' and accepted the broad differences reflected by
> streaming. The questions I put to the pupils confirmed this
> recognition. I would not put any great weight on the answers,
> but record them since they suggest the inarticulate case that
> the children cannot themselves put. The answers imply that
> the streaming process controls friendships and tightens the
> groups further, and that some children, accepting the ABC
> hierarchy, aspire to worlds above them, locating good looks
> and ideal friends there.
>
> The school is organised in the traditional spirit that is
> common to most primary school. As we have seen, this means
> that a process of selection by social class, and even by date of
> birth, is taking place. It means too that the school accepts that
> for practical purposes there are roughly three types of chil-
> dren with distinct but different skills. This is not hidden at all,
> and I never had any difficulty in recognising which were 'C'
> classes and which were 'A'; and sometimes I had no difficulty
> in spotting which were 'A' teachers and which were 'C'. The
> twin principles of selection and competition were visible at
> work everywhere (p.71).

A third primary based study conducted by **Barker-Lunn** for the National Foundation for Educational Resarch (Barker-Lunn, J. *Streaming in primary schools* (1970)) returned once again to the basic issue of the relationships between streaming, social class and pupil performance. A mixture of research techniques were employed: (1) the progress of 5,521 pupils in 100 schools was monitored. (2) Data from 36 matched pairs of schools, streamed and unstreamed, were compared. (3) In 14 of these matched pairs the attitudes of pupils and parents were measured. (4) Six schools, three streamed and three non-streamed, were selected for 'further more intensive study'. (5) Three schools making the change from streaming to non-streaming were examined as case studies. We do not have the space here to consider the twenty major findings of the project, but in several respects Barker-Lunn moved beyond the previous studies quoted, in particular in pointing to the crucial relationships between teacher attitudes to streaming and their teaching methods. Teachers who were in favour of streaming but were working in non-streamed schools 'appeared to create a "streamed atmosphere" within their non-streamed classes'.

Streaming in secondary schools

What was happening as a result of these studies was that far more attention was being paid by researchers to the effects of school organisation and teachers' behaviour and attitudes upon pupils' school careers, and a valid case was being established for the use of case study research to illuminate these issues. However, the major breach in the dominant quantitative approach in educational research came with the publication of two case studies of streamed boys' secondary schools, Hargreaves's *Social Relations in a Secondary School* (Hargreaves, D.H. (1967)) based on Lumley secondary modern school, and Lacey's *Hightown Grammar* (Lacey, C. (1970)). In particular the importance of these studies lies in the theoretical and conceptual developments that they provide in their accounts of and explanations for the workings and effects of streaming.

Both studies identify and plot the processes of differentiation and polarisation which are associated with the separation of pupils into streams. Differentiation is the teachers' 'categorisation' of pupils according to perceived differences in academic performance and behaviour. Pupils who valued academic success and pursued it and who conformed to the teacher's demands were positively evaluated and favourably perceived by their teachers, while those who were unable or unwilling to conform were negatively evaluated and perceived. Lacey goes on to define the concomitant process of polarisation in the following way:

> Polarisation, on the other hand, takes place within the student body, partly as a result of differentiation, but influenced by external factors and with an autonomy of its own. It is a process of sub-culture formation in which the school-dominated, normative culture is opposed by an alternative culture which I refer to as the 'anti-group' culture. The content of the anti-group culture will, of course, be very much influenced by the school and its social setting. For example, it may range from a folk music CND group in a minor public school to a delinquent sub-culture at a secondary modern school in an old urban area. In Hightown Grammar School it fell between these extremes and was influenced by the large working-class and Jewish communities of Hightown (p.57).

The emergence of an anti-school orientation among those pupils who are allocated to low-stream positions is manifested both in the attitudes and behaviour of the pupils, and in the development of antipathies between them and those who remain committed to the norms and values sponsored by the teachers. High status in the top-stream classes is associated with the formal system of academic success and failure, the successful pupils are the most popular. In the lower streams status is related to the informal system of pupil values. The most popular boys are those who celebrate their opposition to school and their teachers by bad behaviour, not doing work, truanting and 'being tough'.

The impact of streaming

Both Lacey and **Hargreaves** argue that those pupils who are allocated to low streams suffer a degradation of self. Their sense of self worth is undermined. Their person is literally under attack. Inasmuch as the dominant official values in the school reinforce and reward academic achievement, allocation to a low stream is allocation to a position of inferior status. It is a label of failure. The experience of failure, both as a result of the streaming system itself, and of the reinforcement of this in the negative perceptions held by the teachers in their daily work with low-stream pupils, leads these pupils to search for alternative bases on which to establish their self-esteem. The most readily available alternatives lies in the inversion of the schools' values. The low-stream anti-school cultures thus derive their initial coherence from being opposed to the values to which the teachers give importance. Clearly, such anti-school cultures are also invested with elements of working-class culture (as Willis describes) and media-relayed teenage cultures (punk rock, skinheads, etc.).

It is in the grammar school that the effects of streaming are perhaps most clear cut in terms of their impact on the social lives and sense of personal worth of the pupils. All the Hightown pupils came to the school on the basis of 11+ success, yet within a short time in the highly competitive atmosphere, some found themselves for the first time labelled as failures. The effects were in some cases drastic: sleeplessness, bed wetting, headaches and other physical reactions were not uncommon. By year two a significant proportion of the pupils were markedly anti-school in their attitudes and behaviour as they adjusted socially to their new status and experiences of failure.

It is also in the grammar school that a clear-cut relationship was to be found between the internal selection processes and the social class of the pupils. Middle-class pupils were over-presented in the top-stream classes in the initial allocation, and this relationship became increasingly close over time. Furthermore, Lacey is able to demonstrate a subtle interplay between home and school factors at work in the long-term construction of pupil careers, related to the 'cultural resources' of the family unit. These resources were particularly crucial in attempts to reprieve failure. He portrays parents and pupil competing as a team for scarce rewards. Clearly, many working-class parents found themselves handicapped in this competition in not having had personal experience of the demands of a grammar school education, in Bourdieu's terms such families lacked 'cultural capital'.

The new sociology of schooling

The work of Lacey and Hargreaves played a significant part in re-orienting research in the sociology of education, school-based and classroom-based studies became increasingly popular during the early 1970s. Sharp and Green, and Willis, were clearly influenced by the new methods pioneered by Lacey and Hargreaves, and there is now a second generation of school case studies which follows on directly from Lumley and Hightown. Woods' (1979) study of Lowfield Secondary Modern, Burgess' (1983) of Bishop Macgregor Comprehensive and my own (Ball 1981) of *Beachside Comprehensive,* are probably most often referred to.

Beachside in particular takes up the concern with the effects of forms of grouping on pupil performance and 'ability' and compares banding (a form of streaming) with mixed-ability grouping. The separation of the Beachside pupils into bands was also, in effect, a separation into different institutional sub-worlds within the totality of the school. These separate sub-worlds provided radically different experiences of schooling for the pupils. Differences were apparent in the forms of subject knowledge presented to them, in the methods of teaching employed, and in the nature of teacher-pupil relationships. In the long term the allocation to bands and the different educational experiences which followed are related directly to the distribution of occupational opportunity and future life chances. There is some support here for Bowles and Gintis' notion of differential correspondence (see Chapter 3). Again low band pupils were regarded as failures. Again their adjustment to inferior status produced a vociferous anti-school culture which made their classes difficult, sometimes impossible, to teach. Differentiation and polarisation were starkly in evidence.

However, the introduction of mixed-ability classes to replace banding involved the removal of many of the organisational aspects of differentiation and polarisation at Beachside. And the new form of grouping clearly inhibited the development of anti-school behaviour as a result. Pupils were no longer faced with the problem of failure through allocation to low bands, social classes were mixed and classroom experiences shared. Despite these changes however the data also suggested that academic differentiation was still taking place and that as a result some features of the banding system were reproduced within the mixed-ability classes. Over time the relationship between social class and academic performance became increasingly obvious, success roles in the classroom (best marks, top of the class etc.) being dominated by middle-class pupils. Middle-class pupils were as a result much more likely to gain access to O-level as opposed to CSE courses at 14+.

All of the studies referred to here carry the basic concern with describing and explaining social-class inequalities into the micro-sociological arena of the school. In a sense, the 'blame' for working-class failure (and to an extent female failure) was being shifted from 'feckless parents' to 'biased teachers'. Some commentators have described these studies as involved in 'teacher-bashing'. While the interactionist researchers tended to see teachers as culpable discriminators, the Marxists analysts, as we have seen, view them as unwitting agents of capitalism. Clearly, neither view is totally accurate but the focus on classroom interaction has identified a number of ways in which inequalities are directly produced through teacher-pupil interaction.

Boys and girls in the classroom

It is clear from a number of studies that boys and girls have very different sorts of classroom experiences. For example, the findings of an American study by Good, Sikes and Brophy (1973), based upon interactions recorded in seventh and eighth-grade classrooms (pupils aged 13 and 14) found significant differences in the amount and type of contact which boys and girls received from their teachers.

> . . . with a single exception, boys received more of all types of interactions than girls. The boys themselves initiated more questions and contacts with teachers, called out more answers, and guessed more frequently than girls.
>
> Teachers, reciprocally, provided boys with more response opportunities. Boys received more questions of all kinds. Interestingly, boys as a group received both more positive and more negative affect from teachers. . . When teachers do express affect toward girls, it is more likely to be positive.

In summary, boys were provided with more opportunities to respond in the classroom and more teacher affect (both positive and negative) was directed at them. Boys were also found to create more response opportunities for themselves.

Good, T., Sikes, J. and Brophy, J. 'Effects of teacher sex and student sex on classroom interaction', *Journal of Educational Psychology*, (1973) 65, 1, pp.74–87.

However, Good *et al.* also point out that when teachers' rankings of pupil achievement are taken into account, significant differences can be found in the quality and quantity of classroom interaction experienced by low-achieving compared with high-achieving boys. In other words, gender is not the only aspect of inequality at work in classroom interaction. Stanworth's (1983) study of A-level classes offers broad support for the analysis of Good *et al.*, although she examines only gender-related factors and not differences associated with level of achievement. She reports that, from the pupils' point of view, it is boys who stand out vividly in classroom interaction.

Boys are, according to the pupils' reports, four times more likely than girls to join in discussion, or to offer comments in class. They are twice as likely to demand help or attention from the teacher, and twice as likely to be seen as 'model pupils'.

More importantly, it seems to pupils that boys receive the lion's share of teachers' attention and regard. Boys are, on pupils' accounts:

Slightly more likely to be the pupils for whom teachers display most concern.

Twice as likely to be asked questions by teachers.

Twice as likely to be regarded by teachers as highly conscientious.

Twice as likely to be those with whom teachers get on best.

Three times more likely to be praised by teachers (and slightly more likely to be criticised).

Three times more likely to be the pupils whom teachers appear to enjoy teaching.

Five times more likely to be the ones to whom teachers pay most attention. (p.33)

These sorts of differences were of equal relevance in the classes taught by women teachers. Boys were still the focus of attention. In addition, teachers reported that they identified more readily with boys and were more attached to them. They were more likely to reject girls and often assumed routinely that they would not pursue their studies because of marriage.

The implications of such differences in attitude and interaction are not just a matter of unequal access to scarce resources, and teachers' time and attention. Learning in the classroom is not limited solely to the content of the official curriculum. The 'form' of schooling also 'teaches' through what is sometimes referred to as the 'hidden curriculum'. Messages and signals are transmitted to pupils through the organisation and practices of the school. Pupils learn their place in the order of things. They learn those subjects and behaviours that are valued and those that are not. They learn how to get by. This is the moral curriculum. All teaching carries with it a moral component. For example, the preparation of pupils for examinations tends to encourage a sense of competition between individuals. They learn to view knowledge as private property, to be kept to themselves and not shared with others. Examinations also lead to an emphasis on memorisation as opposed to understanding and on facts rather than principles. The pupil is learning about learning.

Coping with the classroom

Classroom research has also been addressed to other aspects of teacher–pupil interaction. Woods for example, has published a number of papers which explore the pupils' 'perceptions of and handling of classroom issues and teachers' demands'. He has analysed the sorts of negotiations that take place 'as teachers seek to maximise pupils' efforts, and pupils often to minimise them' (Woods 1983, p.225), and the responses of pupils to teachers' various attempts to control them. 'If teachers do not collude with them, and connive at the "working game" . . . pupils will sometimes take the initiative in transforming the activity of work into an activity of play. Thus there is a great deal of playing at working, and playing at listening' (p.231). And recently Measor and Woods (1984) have plotted in some detail the processes of social adaptation and mutual adjustment that go on as pupils move from primary school into the first year of secondary schooling. Again they highlight negotiation and compromise:

> In the formal area of school life, pupils had to discover the working rules, but at least there was a strongly articulated framework to begin with as a basis. Teachers set up the frame and pupils reacted. In the informal area, pupils had to make their own running in several different arenas. They had three major issues to cope with: (i) relationships with their classmates; (ii) the pressures that derived from the informal culture; (iii) cross-gender relationships and adolescent sexuality. They had no explicit formulae to guide them other than the comparatively vague intimations from siblings, older friends and, of course, rumour and myth. This uncertainty and lack of structure increased pupil anxiety in this area (p.61).

Meanwhile, Hargreaves (1984), among others, has sought to develop an analysis of the strategies that teachers employ in dealing with the demands and travails of classroom work.

> How teachers organise pupil learning experiences and evaluate them would seem to be an important topic for investigation. Why teachers organise and evaluate pupil learning and behaviour in one way rather than another would also seem to qualify as a question worth asking. If we pursue this latter question then we need to explore how the pedagogical strategies which teachers employ are meaningful responses to experienced problems, constraints and dilemmas. We need to consider the possibility that teachers construct the world of the classroom through the employment of different teaching styles but that this process of construction occurs perhaps in situations not of their own choosing and that there are a set of constraints in play which require some sort of resolution through the decisions that teachers are daily and repeatedly called on to make (pp.65–66).

Hargreaves' dubs these resolutions 'coping strategies', a concept which links the immediate micro-sociological context, the classroom and its demands, with the macro-sociological context of constraints and demands within which the classroom is set. Coping strategies are creative responses to the dual limitations of situation and social structure.

Between schools

In some ways it is a natural step from case studies of individual schools to the comparison of schools and their effects on pupils. Do certain forms of organisation or school regime produce 'better' outcomes than others? Or are schools primarily a reflection of the characteristics of their pupil intake?

American research, notably Coleman (1966) and Jencks (1972), have found, on the side of the intake, that it is the social class and home background of the pupils that explains the differences between schools. However, recent British research has given much greater emphasis to the effects of schools on their pupils. Reynolds (1976) has investigated the effects of different types of school regime on the behaviour, in and out of school, of their pupils. Schools which attempted to maintain strict and extensive control over all aspects of their pupils – described by Reynolds as 'refusing a truce' – were associated with higher levels of truancy and court convictions and lower levels of going on to further education, than schools which were willing to negotiate with their pupils and which operated a less punitive disciplinary system.

> It is worth saying quite simply that the evidence from these schools suggests that the more a school seeks high control over its more senior pupils by increasing organisational compulsion and decreasing pupil autonomy, the more these pupils may regard their schools as maladjusted to their needs. Rebellion within and delinquency without will be the result of the failure of the pupils and their teachers to declare a truce.
>
> Reynolds (1976) p.226.

Rutter *et al.* (1979) have taken school effectiveness research a stage further, exploring both intake variables and school variables. They found the latter to be of major significance. Outcomes could not be predicted from intake data alone. Despite the use of a whole variety of measurable organisational indices (size of classes, quality of buildings, forms of grouping), greatest emphasis is given in the Rutter research to the much more elusive variable of 'school ethos'. That is to say schools which emphasise the academic, where teachers take care in preparing lessons, turn up to lessons on time, set homework and mark books regularly, appear to establish expectations to which pupils respond with hard work and good behaviour. But Rutter's research does not tell us how or why such attitudes and expectations have their effect on pupils. The itemisation of a variable does little to capture the realities of life in 'successful' as against 'unsuccessful' schools. Research in this area is continuing.

School knowledge

As indicated in the Introduction, there is a second strand of work focused, at least in part, inside the school which attempts to examine the nature of school knowledge. This area of study was intitially identified with **Young** (1971) and derives its impetus from the sociology of knowledge. Some of the concerns here have much in common with the Marxist orientation outlined previously. That is to say, it begins with the assumption that any knowledge is always knowledge from a particular point of view and that school knowledge reflects, for the most part, the interests and concerns of certain powerful groups within society. Thus, in our schools the knowledge that is admitted into the formal curriculum is always a selection from all available knowledge and even in this selection there is a hierarchy among subjects, some (like Maths and English) are generally regarded as high status, others (like Woodwork and Art) are generally seen as low status. Young regards knowledge as stratified, therefore, and he argues that the interests of high-status knowledge will be defended against attempts to introduce new subjects. Pupils will come to accept and add their own weight to the defence of the status quo.

Young is interested in actual knowledge-in-use in his discussion of the school curriculum. He presents the view that knowledge is a social construction, it is socially defined and agreed. Furthermore school knowledge, as knowledge-in-use, is negotiated and mediated at several levels including within the classroom. Even teachers and pupils do not necessarily agree on what should be taught as Mathematics or Technology, even when working within the limitations of an examination syllabus. Knowledge-in-use is therefore the product of the interests of various competing groups. What counts as school Mathematics or school English may actually change over time as new definitions are asserted by powerful advocates.

The curriculum

The prevailing tendency in our schools is the teaching of what Young calls 'curriculum-as-fact'. Knowledge is treated and presented as though it were fixed and immutable and not in any way the product of human agency. He contrasts this with curriculum-as-practice, which can convey an impression of knowledge as responding to human intention but which suffers equally in obscuring the political basis of knowledge definition. Bernstein's work fits in with this through his analysis of the three 'message systems' of the curriculum, which are the views and definitions of knowledge embedded in the structures and processes of the school curriculum. The three 'message systems' are content (what counts as valid knowledge), pedagogy or teaching method (what counts as valid realisation of knowledge), and the assessment of knowledge (what counts as valid evaluation). We can get some grasp of these ideas by again considering the prevailing tendency in our schools (specifically secondary schools).

The 'packaging' of knowledge

Bernstein typifies the secondary-school curriculum in this country as representing a 'collection code'. Knowledge is presented in discrete units, as separate subjects with their own concerns, contents and methods. In other words they are strongly separated off from one another. It is rare to find attempts being made to deal with knowledge, issues or problems across these fixed subject boundaries. Teachers normally specialise in one area only and this reinforces the separation. The learning pupils do is therefore concerned with separate 'chunks' of abstract knowledge, a bit of history, a bit of geography, a bit of science, etc.

Furthermore, what is taught is essentially fact. Students learn the content of a subject rather than its methods. They do not learn its underlying principles. As a result assessment is usually in the form of tests and examinations. What has been learned (or memorised) is regurgitated. This is what is sometimes referred to as the 'banking concept of education'. The teacher makes a series of deposits in the student's mind and at the end of the course makes a withdrawal in the form of an examination. Marks are awarded according to how much of the original deposit remains intact. In effect students do not touch the knowledge and it does not touch them. It is inert. Teaching and learning is thus a one way process, the teacher is all-knowing, the pupil a passive recipient, an empty vessel waiting to be filled up. The relationship is a formal one. As with the relationship between subjects, the teacher–pupil relationship is strongly bounded. The teacher defines what is to be taught, how it is to be taught and how it is to be assessed. (Always bearing in mind the provisos about negotiation mentioned above).

Bernstein goes on to contrast this type of schooling with an 'integrated code', where separate subjects are subordinated to integrating principles, where topics or themes are studied rather than subjects, where underlying principles are taught rather than facts, where understanding rather than recall of knowledge would be tested, and where the teacher–pupil relationship is an interactive learning partnership. Here the emphasis would be on discovery rather than rote learning. The pupil would be actively involved in the learning process.

Criticisms and future research

The considerable body of school-based research conducted during the 1970s and earlier 1980s has done a great deal to 'fill in' the processes of schooling so radically neglected by previous researchers. However, critics of interactionism have argued that the energy and commitment being put into classroom observation and research into pupils lives has had the unfortunate effect of drawing attention away from the structural and historical constraints upon schooling. Interactionist research does emphasise the social strategies of actors rather than the determining influences of social structure. But clearly an adequate sociological account of schooling needs to recognise both. The work of Hargreaves, mentioned above, is one attempt to link structure and action, but it is likely that the dispute over where the theoretical emphasis should lie will continue for some time. The sociology of education continues to change and develop, it is not a static body of 'dead' knowledge but rather a lively field of endeavour (empirical and theoretical), involving a constant interchange of new ideas, new research and new problems.

PART 3

Statistical data and documentary readings

6 Statistics on education

School and social mobility

The study *Origins and Destinations* is an attempt to examine the pattern of educational inequalities and the effects of educational reform in the period 1945–1970. It is based on a massive sample of 10 000 men living in England and Wales in 1972. (One of the obvious criticisms of the study is the absence of any data on women). In particular, the study examines the tripartite system and private sector in terms of class differences in access to education and asks the question 'How far has the British education system achieved its professed goal of meritocracy?' Table 6.1 is one attempt to test Bourdieu's concept of 'cultural capital' (discussed in Chapter 4). One hypothesis which can be derived from Bourdieu's analysis is that children (in this case sons) will follow in the educational footsteps of their parents, thus ensuring a high degree of self-recruitment between genera-tions of social class groups, or in this case 'education classes'. Looking at the diagonal cells in the Table there seems to be fairly strong support for the self-recruitment hypothesis. The non-selective group is particularly insular, 71.7 per cent of sons of parents who attended non-selective schools also attended non-selective schools. The figures in brackets indicate the extent of social mobility, thus 20.5 per cent of the sample came from what Halsey *et al.* call 'uneducated families' and entered state selective schools. This was a period of expansion in educational provision in the state sector and some upward mobility is to be expected, almost 25 per cent in all. Only eight per cent of the sample were downwardly mobile. In this period then, with secondary provi-

Table 6.1

Parents' and respondents' secondary schooling

Parental schooling	Private schools	State selective	Non-selective	All
One of both parents attended private secondary schools[1] (N = 383)	47.7 (2.2)*	31.1 (1.4)	21.1 (0.9)	99.9 (4.5)
One or both attended state selective schools (N = 1204)	11.7 (1.7)	44.7 (6.3)	43.6 (6.2)	100.0 (14.2)
Both parents attended non-selective schools (N = 6923)	3.1 (2.5)	25.2 (20.5)	71.7 (58.3)	100.0 (81.3)
All (N = 8510)	(6.4)	(28.2)	(65.4)	(100.0)

[1] Where one parent attended a private secondary school and the other attended a state selective school, the parental schooling has been coded as private.

* Figures in brackets give the cell or marginal frequency as a percentage of the total.

Source: from Halsey, A.H., Heath, A.F. and Ridge, J.M., Origins and Destinations, Clarendon Press, Oxford, (1980) p.76.

sion expanding, the 'cycle of privilege' through selective and private schooling is by no means clear cut. A large proportion of secondary school places were being taken up by boys from 'uneducated families'. The question is then whether this puts them in the position of acquiring 'cultural capital' through schooling or that their lack of 'cultural capital' disadvantages them inside the school. Lacey's (1970) *Hightown Grammar* (discussed in Chapter 5) suggests the latter to be the case. Certainly Halsey *et al.* find that working–class boys were more likely than their middle–class colleagues to leave school early (see Table 6.2). But of those who stay on two–thirds obtain some academic credential, which would seem to call into question Bourdieu's notion of 'perfect' reproduction. On the other hand *Origins and Destinations* may lack the kind of fine grain analysis of educational experiences that a true test of Bourdieu's work would require:

Table 6.2

Social class and school examinations
Grammar school pupils only

Father's social class	Percentage staying on until 16 or later	Percentage obtaining school certificate or one or more O-levels
I.II. (Upper middle class) N = 376	92.8	83.2
III,IV,V (Lower middle class) N = 484	82.9	71.9
VI,VII,VIII (Working class) N = 495	78.4	63.2

Source: adapted from *Origins and Destinations*, p.145.

Table 6.3

School leavers during the academic year 1981–82
Destination on leaving and type of school – England only

Percentage boys and girls	Comprehensive	Grammar	Other secondary	Total	Independent schools	All schools
Degree Courses	5.94	28.04	1.05	6.25	36.15	8.02
Teacher training courses	0.40	1.88	0.12	0.43	0.80	.45
Other FE courses	18.50	25.31	22.61	19.01	30.49	19.69
Permanent employment	64.14	37.59	66.85	63.53	23.22	61.15
Not known	11.02	7.18	9.37	10.78	9.34	10.69
Total	100.00	100.00	100.00	100.00	100.00	100.00

Source: adapted from Department of Education and Science, Statistics of Education, London, HMSO, (1979).

School and inequalities

Table 6.3 gives a very crude impression of the very different educational routes and opportunities provided by the different sectors of the education system. Here we still find grammar schools existing within a predominantly comprehensive system, indeed there were 632 850 comprehensive school leavers in 1981–82 as against 21 570 grammar school leavers. However, the relative privilege of the grammar school route remains clear; grammar school leavers are nearly five times more likely to be going on to degree courses (5.94 per cent as against 28.04 per cent). An even higher proportion of Independent school leavers go on to higher education (36.15 per cent), while the average across all schools is only 8.02 per cent. Comprehensive and other secondary school leavers are most likely to go straight into employment, 64.14 per cent and 66.85 per cent respectively. More recent figures would undoubtedly indicate a decline in the proportion of leavers in this category as a result of increased youth unemployment and the provision of training courses through YTS etc.

The interesting point in Table 6.4 is the overall increase, across the period covered, in each category. In simple terms schools were apparently becoming more successful in getting pupils through examinations, the percentage of pupils leaving school without any qualifications whatsovever has virtually halved (from 21.6 per cent to 11.2 per cent). This provides a notable counterpoint to the claims made during the 1970s, by many critics of comprehensive schooling, that comprehensive reorganisation would lead to an inevitable decline in educational standards. From these rather simple indicators the reverse seems to be the case. But the question remains as to whether examination achievements should be the only or the most important criterion to use when evaluating the performance of schools.

We must be careful in interpreting Table 6.5 because we are working with raw numbers rather than percentages. Part of the increase in numbers of pupils passing O–level and CSE grade 1 in these subjects is the result of a sheer increase in cohort numbers, the numbers of pupils in each year group. What is most stiking about these figures is the comparison between boys and girls. They reflect a clear division between maths and science on the one hand and English and modern languages on the

Table 6.4

Attainments of school leavers 1972–73 to 1981–2 in State schools

	1972–73	1973–74	1974–75	1975–76	1976–77	1977–78	1978–79	1979–80	1980–81	1981–82
Percentage of all leavers with 1 or more A-levels		12.5	12.4	12.8	12.7	12.7	12.6	12.6	13.5	14.1
With no A-level passes but higher grade O-level and CSE results[1]										
5 or more		8.2	7.8	8.0	8.8	8.8	9.1	9.1	9.2	9.9
1–4		24.9	26.0	26.4	27.3	27.2	27.8	27.7	27.3	27.3
With no higher grade O-level or CSE results but one or more other grades[2]		32.8	33.9	35.3	35.5	36.2	37.0	37.8	38.0	37.5
No GCE or CSE qualifications		21.6	19.8	17.5	15.7	15.0	13.6	12.8	12.0	11.2

[1] O-level grades A–C and CSE grade 1.
[2] O-level grades D–E and CSE grades 2–5.

Source: adapted from Department of Education and Science, *Statistics of Education*, London, HMSO, (1979).

Table 6.5

Subject analysis of GCE O-level and CSH higher grade achievements

		1977–78	1978–79	1979–80	1980–81	1981–82
		Thousands				
English	boys	117.71	119.01	121.24	119.93	127.38
	girls	148.71	151.23	154.07	153.75	162.24
Maths	boys	105.95	110.06	112.03	112.30	119.50
	girls	74.87	80.27	85.18	87.48	94.65
Science	boys	124.82	128.07	130.26	129.11	135.84
	girls	77.81	80.77	85.10	86.18	92.47
Modern	boys	43.50	44.21	44.30	44.59	46.70
Languages	girls	63.06	66.64	68.58	68.82	75.16

Source: adapted from Department of Education and Science, *Statistics of Education*, London, HMSO, (1979).

other, with boys more successful in the former and girls more successful in the latter. Two factors are at work here. First, when pupils select their subject options at 14+, boys are much more likely to choose, and be accepted for, science courses. Science subjects, excepting biology, are stereotypically thought of as a male preserve (we can see this in the figures for university courses below), preparing for and leading to male careers (see the extract from Measor 1984, p.95). Languages and language skills are more commonly identified with girls and female careers (translators, secretaries, couriers, air hostesses – all interestingly service jobs). Second, while most schools require all pupils to continue with english and mathematics courses until 16+, there is still a notable difference in the successes of girls in english and boys in mathematics, and again this is reflected in choices for university courses. This suggests that curriculum and classroom processes are at work in gender differentiation.

Table 6.6

University subjects studied in 1982–83 analysed by domicile and sex

| Undergraduates | | Percentage of total who were: | | |
Subject group	Total (000s)	Home men	Home women	Overseas students
Education	3.8	27	61	12
Medicine, dentistry and health	28.2	52	43	5
Engineering and technology	36.5	77	7	16
Agriculture, forestry and veterinary science	5.1	60	38	2
Biological and physical sciences	59.3	63	31	5
Administrative, business and social studies	58.5	52	41	7
Architecture and other professional and vocational studies	4.1	57	33	10
Language, literature and area studies	32.0	30	67	3
Arts, other than languages	22.4	44	52	5
All subjects	250.0	55	38	7

Source: adapted from Department of Education and Science, *Statistics of Education*, London, HMSO, (1979).

In Table 6.6 we can again see a clear pattern of gender related subject choices. Men predominate in engineering and technology, agriculture and related subjects, the sciences and architecture and other professional and vocational studies. Women predominate in education and language and literature. The other areas are more evenly split but men are in the majority in medicine and women in other arts subjects. Overall, considering the home students only, 59 per cent of students are men, 41 per cent are women. This is actually a worsening of the position of women which resulted from the cuts in home student number targets announced by the UGC (University Grants Committee) in 1981, and the associated shift in resources from arts to science subjects. As the number of places available in universities is reduced then women candidates tend to do less well in obtaining places. This cut in numbers is summarised in Table 6.7.

Table 6.7

Subjects studied by full-time students: 1977–78 to 1982–83

	1977–78 (000s)	1981–82 (000s)	1982–83 (000s)	Percentage change since 1977–78	1981–82
Undergraduates					
Arts students	111.5	120.7	117.7	6	−2
Science students	98.4	109.6	109.1	11	−1
Medicine/dentistry students	21.7	23.1	23.3	6	1
Postgraduates					
Arts students	25.0	24.5	23.2	−7	−5
Science students	21.6	19.6	19.5	−9	−1
Medicine/dentistry students	2.3	2.7	2.6	12	−3

Source: adapted from Department of Education and Science, *Statistics of Education,* London, HMSO, (1979).

It is also useful to examine university entrants in relation to social class and race/ethnicity. This can be done in terms of APRs (Age Participation Rates). That is the percentage of the 18+ age group of any social group which gain access to university.

Table 6.8

Age participation rates in universities in Great Britain 1981–82

Overall APR for male students	15.1%
Overall APR for female students	11.8%
APR for middle-class students	27%
APR for working-class students	7%
APR for ethnic minority students	3%

Source: composite table from several sources.

This means that while 27 per cent of middle-class 18 year olds gain university places, only five per cent of working-class 18 year olds do so, and three per cent of 18 years olds from ethnic minority groups do so. This is a massive underrepresentation of the working-class and ethnic minority students. Girls are also less successful than boys at gaining places.

Table 6.9 illustrates a further aspect of gender related inequality in school, this time concerning teachers. Women teachers are underrepresented at in all positions in school except for the two most junior, scales 1 and 2. It is often argued that the lack of female role models in senior positions in schools is one of the factors that tends to depress the achievements and aspirations of girl pupils.

As noted in the main text, examination results are difficult to interpret and straightforward comparisons are often dangerous. At face value Table 6.10 shows the Inner London Education Authority to have both the highest level of secondary school expenditure per pupil and the highest proportion of unqualified school leavers. On the other hand other indicators on the table show the ILEA performance in a more favourable light. Either way there are a whole range of factors relating to pupil characteristics and environmental conditions which need to be taken into account. For example: over a quarter of ILEA pupils come from single parent families, well above the national average; over one third of ILEA pupils qualify for a free school meal, roughly twice the national average; and English is not the first language of one in six ILEA pupils, a total of 147 different languages are spoken among ILEA pupils. One conclusion might be that any reduction in expenditure on education would inevitably lead to a reduction in measurable attainments.

Table 6.9

Sex distribution – teachers in all Inner London Education Authority secondary schools (1982–3)

	Head teacher	Deputy	Senior teacher	Scale 4	Scale 3	Scale 2	Scale 1	Total
Male	60.2% (106)	56.6% (210)	65.1% (262)	59.9% (950)	81.1% (1,041)	46.5% (1,107)	42.1% (1,332)	49.5% (5,008)
Female	39.8% (70)	43.3% (161)	34.3% (137)	40.1% (636)	48.9% (995)	53.3% (1,275)	57.9% (1,831)	50.5% (5,105)

Source: from ILEA, Improving Secondary Schools: Report of the Committee on the Curriculum and Organisation of Secondary Schools, (1984) p.99.

Table 6.10

Examination results and educational expenditure in urban education authorities

	percentage of school leavers with no graded result	percentage of school leavers with one or more higher grade passes at O-level or CSE	percentage of school leavers with five or more higher grade passes at O-level or CSE	Secondary school expenditure per pupil pounds
ILEA	22.6	40.6	13.7	1,234.1
Manchester	22.2	40.0	15.5	1,065.3
Birmingham	16.2	43.8	17.2	873.6
Liverpool	20.0	41.7	15.8	968.3
Barking	20.2	38.7	11.2	932.4
Wolverhampton	17.8	40.7	13.6	912.2
Knowlsley	20.9	36.6	11.7	923.4

Source: adapted from DES *Statistical Bulletin*, December 1983.

Discussion questions on statistics

1 Tables 6.1 and 6.2 from *Origins and Destinations* illustrate the gap which exists between 'formal' and 'effective' opportunity in education. While large numbers of working-class pupils from 'uneducated families' gained access to grammar schools after 1944, they were clearly less likely to be successful in such schools than their middle-class colleagues. Drawing on the material from Chapters 4 and 5 what factors deriving from 'home' and 'school' can you suggest to account for this.

2 Considering the pattern of results presented in Table 6.4 what sorts of changes in schooling could be cited to explain the increases in examination attainment? Obviously anything you put forward here can only be a matter of hypothesis. It is virtually impossible to directly link general organisational or curricular changes with overall changes in examination performance.

3 Table 6.5 shows the effects of gender differentiation in the secondary school curriculum. List the range of school factors which might conspire to produce these effects. It might be helpful if you construct the list under separate headings – the curriculum, teacher behaviour, teacher attitudes, parental expectations and pupil pressures.

4 Table 6.6 may be taken as an indicator of the status hierarchy which exists among subject areas in higher education. What factors can you suggest at work in creating and perpetuating this hierarchy? The discussion of Michael Young's work in Chapter 5 may be of help in this.

5 What sort of differences in family life (values, language, childrearing and culture) might be employed to account for the differences in Age Participation Rates presented in Table 6.8? You should consider the importance of differences which affect social class, race *and* gender, in other words differences within and between families in the aspirations, attitudes and experiences directed at children.

6 How would you explain the distribution of teachers recorded in Table 6.9? What effects might this distribution have on pupils' aspirations and attitudes regarding possible employment? What effects might this distribution have on the career commitments and aspirations of women teachers?

7 If you were required to defend the higher level of expenditure

ture per pupil indicated in the case of ILEA in Table 6.10 what case would you put forward? Can you identify any significant variations in the pattern of school performance presented in the Table? In general terms what does the Table tell us about the relationship between expenditure and examination performance? Can you suggest any alternative to examination performance as measures of effective schooling?

7 Documentary readings

In this chapter we will look at some recent writing in the sociology of education. The extracts presented below highlight some of the themes and issues introduced in the previous chapters.

Reading 1 Roger Dale: Thatcherism and education

This philosophy appears to be directly rooted in Mrs Thatcher's own personal experience, and, we might add, in those of Rhodes Boyson and Norman Tebbit, too. There is little respect here for those Tory grandees and paternalists who preach a form of universalism without ever having to experience its dirty end. There is little readiness to dole out equal benefits to those who are going to make good use of them and those who will just squander them. There is a distinct reluctance to support those unwilling or unable to support themselves, especially if it means that there is less for the deserving. And so, Thatcherite education policy might be seen as not so much anti-statist as anti-universalist and anti-social democratic. While the state is to be rolled back – or at least cut back – that is to be done selectively. Thatcherism is very much in favour of selectiveness, of allowing the natural differences between people to grow, both as a reward to the talented and successful, the intellectually and moraly deserving, and as a spur to the less well-endowed, successful or responsible, to make the most of what they have. This spur is signally absent from a universalistic, social democratic Welfare State.

This does not mean that the approach is not anti-statist. Far from it. The market is to be preferred to the state at all points because the desired stratifying power and mechanism are intrinsic to its operations. The market ensures that the best is available to those, and only those, who deserve or can afford it, and that those who neither deserve nor can afford anything else end up with the worst, or nothing, or what is left.

> Dale, R. 'Thatcherism and education' in Ahier, J., and
> Flude, M. (eds.), *Contemporary Education Policy,* Croom Helm,
> London, (1983) pp.249–250.

Here Dale is pointing out some of the crucial themes and contradictions within contemporary Government education policy. There has been a consistent programme of privatisation within educaiton since 1979 and several measures enacted which have introduced competition between schools. Thatcherism stands for individual competition and individual responsibility. The Conservatives are highly suspicious of the Welfare State and what they see as the resulting disincentives for individual competition and initiative. Ironically, however, changes, in education are being brought about by an unprecedented degree of government intervention. Thus, Dale characterises Thatcherism as anti-democratic but not anti-statist; the state remains as a powerful tool for policy implementation.

Reading 2   Paul Corrigan: resistance to schooling

In trying to come to terms with these different methods of control within the school it is easy to see why the one most constantly used, that of constant surveillance, led me to the seemingly incongruous analogy of guerrilla warfare for behaviour in the school. That there was conflict became obvious; that this conflict was not *resolved* by the use of the power of the teacher and the law was equally obvious. The question became, 'What is the source of the power which challenges the teacher?' Youthful exuberance would have wilted early on in the battle; the schoolboy naughtiness of the *Beano* would not have lasted the first use of headmasterly power. It is explicable only in terms of the complete refusal to allow oneself to be taken over by the ideology of the school, and the use of superior numbers to run the teachers into the ground. These different sorts of power began to coincide very clearly with the different sorts of power exercised in a guerrilla struggle: a heavy amount of state power is overwhelming in itself but it has to be made to have its effect; the response to this comes from a larger number of individuals who occasionally act together, but mainly act passively against this power, attempting to reject its effect. The guerrilla forces act within their own ideology of resistance, one which is usually deemed as irrational by the state powers; they use heartlands from which to attack the state power, heartlands which are mainly inaccessible to the agents of the state. For a long time in all these struggles, unless there is intrusion from outside, a position of stalemate can become normal, with each side winning the occasional victory, imposing the occasional set of casualities. Teachers and pupils in secondary schools at the moment will recognise this analogy as a day-to-day reality.

Corrigan, P., *Schooling the Smash Street Kids,* Macmillan, London, (1979) pp.70–71.

Corrigan's analysis of the misbehaviour and disruption caused by working-class pupils in a Sunderland comprehensive school, pupils he calls the Smash Street Kids, leads him to identify this as a form of resistance to schooling. He sees the pupils as defending themselves against the imposition of schooling. The struggles in the classroom, apparently trivial and irrational, are, he argues, indicators of a much greater struggle between the state and subordinate classes in society. You should see similarities here with Willis' work.

Reading 3   The Centre for Contemporary Cultural Studies: the rise of the Manpower Services Commission

The MSC took as it co-ordinates an already established 'world of work'. Certainly the MSC re-presented this world ideologically, making it, for example, more 'open' to young workers than it was and making unemployment appear as a product of individual inadequacies rather than as an endemic consequence of the capitalist mode of production. But this re-presentation did not mean that the MSC lacked, in practice, an accurate assessment of some needs of capitalism. The MSC took existing divisions between employers and workers, between different 'types' of worker and between workers with different 'interests' (particularly male and female workers) for granted. Where the MSC broke new ground was in the tightness of the link which it established between the needs of employers (both logical and perceived) and state provision.

The commission took the differentiation already achieved

by schooling as its datum line, and concentrated its attention on those who left school at 16. The young worker, or worker to be, was taken as an already constituted category and, within this, the MSC fostered further differentiation. At the most passive this was by allowing 'interests' to run their 'natural' course so that, for example, adult male workers received 75 per cent of places on TOPS schemes concentrated in skill centres and employers' establishments, while female workers were concentrated in FE colleges. This reproduced the division between engineering, construction and automotive occupations and clerical, commercial and hairdressing work. Clerical and commercial 'skills' were in any case being subjected to rapid 'deskilling'. The MSC provision similarly reproduced hierarchies of 'ability' ranging from workers equipped only with 'social and life skills', through workers trained to operator/semi-skilled level, to workers trained with similar technical competences as apprenticed 'craftsmen'. This differentiation carried with it another key concern – the need to discourage many people from acquiring conceptual and critical skills. The MSC both provided work socialisation for many young people who would not otherwise have received it and fostered the attitudes conducive to 'responsible autonomy' – the cheapest and most efficient mode of labour discipline.

CCCS, *Unpopular Education,* Hutchinson, London, (1981) pp.237–38.

The CCCS analysis of the MSC concentrates here on the ways in which existing hierarchies and inequalities are being reproduced and reinforced. The status and gender divisions within the workplace are unquestioningly taken on board in the organisation of MSC schemes. Furthermore, these schemes 'prepare' young people for work by attempting to inculcate attitudes and values regarded as desirable by employers. This sort of analysis extends the 'reproduction theory' beyond school into other spheres of 'education and training'.

Reading 4   Paul Willis: penetrations

. . . this cultural form is not produced by simple outside determination. It is produced also from the activities and

struggles of each new generation. We are dealing with collective, if not consciously directed, will and action as they
overlay, and themselves take up 'creative' positions with
respect to finally reproduce what we call 'outside determinations'. It is these cultural and subjective processes, and actions
which flow from them, which actually produce and reproduce
what we think of as aspects of structure. It is only by passing
through this moment that determinations are made effective
in the social world at all. Decisions are taken by individuals
'freely' and with 'consent' in this realm which no amount of
formal external direction could produce. If working-class kids
on their way to work did not believe the logic of their actions
for themselves, no-one outside, nor outside events, could
convince them – especially in view of the conventional
assessment of what they are doing and where they are going.
The culture provides the principles of individual movement
and action.

The penetrations produced, however, at the cultural level
in the working class by what I still want to call a certain
creativity are by no means quite open ended. They run along
certain lines whose basic determinants lie outside the individual, the group or class. It is no accident that different
groups in different schools, for instance, come up with similar
insights, even though they are the products of separate efforts,
and thus combine to make distinctive class bonds. All the
groups are penetrating through to roughly the same really
determining conditions which hold their present and future
possibilities. The object, therefore, of creativity is something
to be discovered, not imagined. The limits to, and internal
relationships of, what is discovered are already set. In another
society 'the lads' would have been shown the way, they would
not have discovered their own.

Willis, P. <i>Learning to Labour,</i> Saxon House,
Farnborough, (1977) pp.120–121.

In this typically quite difficult passage Willis is discussing the
creativity of the 'counter-school culture' of 'the lads'. He is
suggesting that their insights into the workings of the school
system, their 'penetrations', are in part a creative cultural response and in part a discovery of the commmon objective
conditions of schooling. Structure is translated into action and

belief through the medium of culture. The culture of 'the lads' is liberating but it is also ultimately the vehicle of their subjection to capitalism. In rejecting school, mental labour and the notion of careers 'the lads' condemn themselves to a life of working-class wage labour.

Reading 5   Ivor Goodson: A divisive curriculum

Within the comprehensive schools a clear hierarchy of school subjects developed. The hierarchy was based on the primacy of grammar school subjects which were naturally given such priority by the grammar school staff who largely took over the headships and head of department posts. But the hierarchy was crucially underpinned by patterns of resource allocation. This took place on the basis of assumptions that 'academic' subjects were suitable for 'able' students whilst other subjects were not. These academic subjects were thought to require longer periods to be taught, more highly paid staff and more money for equipment and books. The primacy of academic grammar school subjects was not challenged after comprehensivisation. Hence the 'academic' grammar school subjects and 'able' pupil clienteles continued to enjoy financial priority in the comprehensive school. Separatism of buildings was eliminated, separatism of curricula maintained. Indeed not only did academic subjects retain their dominance; they extended it. From now on, 'academic' rules were extended to the mainstream curriculum of all comprehensive schools.

That comprehensive schools do place overwhelming emphasis on academic examinations, in spite of the growth of ROSLA type courses and pastoral systems, has been recently confirmed in Ball's (1981) study of 'Beachside Comprehensive'. He notes that 'once reorganised as a comprehensive, academic excellence was quickly established as the central tenet of the value system of the school' (p.16); 'academic achievement tended to be the single criterion of success in the school'; and 'teacher resources within the comprehensive school are allocated differently according to the pupils' ability . . . the most experienced teachers spend most of their time with the able pupils' (p.18).

Goodson, I.F. 'Defining a Subject for the Comprehensive School: a case study' in Ball, S.J. (ed.), *Comprehensive Schooling: a reader*, Falmer Press, Lewes, (1984).

The social stratification of schooling, even within the comprehensive school, still owes a great deal to the separate traditions of grammar and elementary schooling. This extract points to the identification of certain types of school knowledge with certain 'types' of pupils (much in the way that was done in the Norwood Report, see Young in Chapter 5). Goodson is also drawing attention to the resource inequalities which often follow from this stratification, the separation of academic from 'non-academic'. Separatism involves the creating of different educational experiences, and different 'life chances', for different groups of pupils.

Reading 6   Rachel Sharp and Anthony Green: social stratification in the classroom

The 'problem' child is in a position of low status which is relatively rigid and binding. His life chances in the classroom, to the extent that he has relatively little contact with the teacher and so is unlikely to alter his identity from that of peculiarity, are severely limited. Being really 'odd' in the teacher's account he has a reified identity to her which is socially structured and reinforced at the classroom level as he has less opportunity to develop contradictory cues and at a wider level, as his identity is accepted by other teachers, parents and social workers. The normal child for this school is in a relatively more fluid position with the chance of moving upward or down the hierarchy of social status to the extent that he or she moves from the low profile position of the normality of adjustment to the routines of busyness.

The élite of the social structure are the few 'bright' children who are able to take most advantage of the 'free day' and 'leading from behind', in that they readily know what it is the teacher wants and can reward the teacher for the time spent with her thus confirming her in her identity as a competent teacher. While the maladjusted or problem child can be used by the teacher as an illustration of the difficulty of her task and the need for this type of approach to pedagogy, so the bright ones can be cited as the operational indicators of the teacher's success, i.e. confident readers, articulate interactors, the child who produces 'interesting', creative work. Thus the structure of pupil stratification illustrates a central paradox of the child-centred approach. In practice, though attempting to generate the lowest possible degree of boundary and hierarchy in pupil identities, social stratification does occur.

> Sharp, R., and Green, A., *Educational and Social Control*,
> Routledge Kegan Paul, London, (1976) pp.124–25.

Here again the theme is social stratification in and through education. The setting here is a 'progressive' primary school and the processes described are occurring within the classroom. Sharp and Green argue that the demands of classroom management lead to a system of pupil typication (bright, average, and odd or abnormal). The teacher interacts differently with and provides different learning opportunities for these different 'types' of pupils. Their long term educational opportunities are thus being delimited very early. Again the major themes here are social reproduction and processes of differentiation.

Reading 7   Stephen Ball: banding and identity

The fact that the pupils came to the secondary school preselected, sorted out into bands, may have been important in making the allocation 'real' to the Beachside teachers. As the band allocation of the pupils was a 'given', a label imposed from ouside prior to any contact with the pupils, the teachers were 'taking', and deriving assumptions on the basis of, that label, rather than 'making' their own evaluation of the relative abilities of individual pupils. Each band–label carries its own particular status within the school and the staff hold preconceived and institutionalised notions about the typical 'band 2 child', the 'remedial child', etc. To a great extent these typifications are bases on what the teacher knows about the bands in terms of their status identity. From the teacher's point of view the behaviour of band 2 forms is 'deviant', contravening their expectations of appropriate classroom behaviour. These labels are consistent and embedded aspects of the system of meanings shared by all the teachers, and are not dependent upon the identification of particular forms or pupils. Once established, the typification 'band 2 form' or 'band 2 pupil' merely awaits the arrival of each new cohort in the school. I am not suggesting that the 'label' of being band 2 in itself creates a 'deviant' identity and is the cause of the 'deviant' acts described previously. But the label of being band 2 imposes certain limitations upon the sort of social identity that may be negotiated by the band 2 pupil. When persons are subjected to a process of categorisation, they are subject also to the imputation of various social identities by virtue of their membership of that category. In this case, it is an identity that involves a status–evaluation and allocation to an inferior position in the status–hierarchy of the school. Band 2 forms, as we shall see, are considered to be 'not up to much academically' and most teachers find them 'unrewarding' to teach. Certainly, by the beginning of the second year in the careers of the case-study forms, it is a label that denotes a behavioural stereotype. The teachers hold stereotypical images of band identity (which I shall refer to as the 'bandness' of pupils). That is, they tend to jump from a single cue or a small number of cues in actual, suspected or alleged behaviour, to a general picture of the 'kind of person with whom one is dealing'.

Ball, S.J., *Beachside Comprehensive,* Cambridge University Press, Cambridge, (1981) pp.36–37.

Persuing the relationship between school processes, teacher perceptions and pupils' opportunities a stage further, this extract from my own research describes the ways in which the organisation of pupil grouping operates to differentiate pupils. These formalised separations build perhaps on identities and labels initiated in the primary school. Despite the theoretical differences in the extracts quoted here there are strong points of common focus and similarities in the analyses put forward.

Reading 8   Lynda Measor: science, gender and identity

One group of girls made an enormous fuss about wearing the spectacles, and made a range of silly jokes on the subject. One girl, Amy, stated that 'they really don't suit me', and decided she would not wear them; she was followed in this rebellion by a number of her friends. The context of this action should be emphasised. The girls were disobeying a very firm and strongly presented instruction given to them by their teacher, who happened to be the headmaster. The girls did this in the second week at their new school, in a situation where circumspect conformity to the demands of the teacher was the norm. The same behaviour was repeated the following week.

Rebecca: I hate wearing these glasses they give me a headache, I had a headache until 4 o'clock yesterday.

Rosemary: Yes it really does give you a headache.

The dislike of wearing the goggles emerged as a central element in Amy's definition of the subject. 'I don't like science, 'cos you have to tie your hair back and wear goggles.' Appearance is, of course, a central issue in the construction of a properly feminine image. . .

. . . The girls, then, had a strong reaction to their science lessons. They had a clear perspective that it involved things that they did not feel it was appropriate or pleasant, or inviting to do. And the 'appropriateness' of that attitude was also recognised by the boys. Kelly's notion of a cluster of attributes that are conventionally labelled masculine or feminine becomes relevant in this context. The girls signalled their objection to the dirt and fumes and smells of science, and also to being asked to look less attractive. They displayed themselves as squeamish, frightened and weak, by their objections to science, and somewhat imcompetent as well, especially in relation to certain kinds of complex machinery and technology. The activities in science contravened conventional views of what 'proper' girls should do, and therefore the girls resisted doing them. The pupils were reading sex-related characteristics into activities and things, and responding to them as a result. This response goes to make their sex-based identity clear to those around them. My suggestion is that the girls actively used aspects of school to construct their identity, in this case their feminine identity. They are not simply responding passively to school in terms of gender stereotypes. Science lessons provided an arena for the acting out of feminine susceptibilities in a public setting. They were a backdrop against which signals could be displayed about feminine identity.

Measor, L., 'Gender and the Sciences: pupil's gender-based conceptions of school subjects', in Hammersley, M., and Hargreaves, A., (eds.) *Curriculum Practice,* Falmer Press, Lewes, (1978) pp.178–79.

Measor's work extends the question of identities and differentiation to the consideration of gender. We have noted already (see Chapter 6) the gender distortions in the pattern of curriculum choices made at 14+. Here Measor illustrates some of the classroom experiences and interplay between boys and girls which together act to produce sex differentiation in the curriculum. But once again the girls here, like Willis' 'lads', contribute to their own exclusion from science by rejecting it as unfeminine and thus threatening to their developing sense of self. Some schools are currently experimenting with single-sex classes in science to avoid just these kinds of effects.

Reading 9 Andy Hargreaves: coping strategies (structure and action)

The message for sociologists of education should be clear. 'Structural' questions and 'interactionist' questions should no longer be dealt with a separate 'issues', each to be covered in their respective fields. Such a false separation will only lead to a continuation of what has been a sad trend in the sociology of education; that of a wild oscillation between two poles of sociological explanation. From systems theories to interpretive brands of sociology and back again to a structurally-based Marxism; almost no time has been spent in taking the opportunity to analyse how classroom matters may relate to the nature of the socio–economic and political structure and the functions which the educational system performs within that structure. Like the gymnast on the trampoline, movement has tended to be up and down between the classroom level and the dizzy structural heights and has rarely provided any degree of forward momentum.

We certainly need to know what goes on in classrooms. But at the same time we need to question, not just in passing but with commitment and with rigour, just what sort of society it is in which we live. We cannot assume that our society is characterised by democratic pluralism even though this might 'fit' nicely with the view that classroom realities are the product of a democratically-based negotiation process. Rather, in a society where wealth is socially produced yet privately appropriated, where increased economic prosperity is paralleled by decreased humanity, and where increased levels of qualification are accompanied by greater opportunities for unemployment, there are grounds for seriously considering or at least confronting a Marxist analysis of contemporary British society, and for exploring how such an analysis might be linked with, an interactionally informed investigation of classroom processes.

Hargreaves, A., 'The significance of classroom strategies', in Hargreaves, A., and Woods, P., (eds.), *Classrooms and Staffrooms*, Open University Press, Milton Keynes, (1984), p.64.

Here then Hargreaves argues for the need for the sociology of education to attempt to synthesise structural and interactionist accounts. In other words, there is a need for accounts of classrooms to recognise the structural processes of social reproduction and the structural limits to action which shape and contain the processes of schooling. Structuralist accounts of education must in turn recognise the degree of autonomy and freedom that exists in schools and thus the extent of structural mismatch between schooling, the economy and the class system.

Discussion questions

As students in school, college or university you have a unique opportunity to pursue issues raised in the text in the most immediate sense. Your own institution can act as a natural laboratory for your investigation of the sociology of education. You can also interrogate your own educational experiences and compare these with those of your colleagues. The questions below are intended to elucidate concepts and ideas dealt with in the text and to prepare you for examination and essay questions you may be confronted with.

Chapter 3

1 Apply Parsons' model of the four functional imperatives to your own institution. How are the four imperatives met? Can you see any problems with this system of analysis as a result of your attempt?

2 Compare the extract quoted from Parsons (p.30) with that from Althusser (p.34). Can you identify any points of similarity and/or major differences between the two in terms of their views on education and its relation to work?

3 Using material from Chapter 5 (i.e. Lacey, Hargreaves and Ball) can you present an alternative explanation for the behaviour and attitudes of Willis' 'lads'? Willis uses the key term 'resistance' and this carries considerable weight in his analysis. Can you see alternative ways of accounting for the behaviour described as 'resistance'?

4 In what ways does the organisation and grouping of students in your institution contribute to 'an unequal distribution of curricular knowledge'? Is there a status hierarchy of knowledge in your institution? What is high status knowledge? What is low status knowledge?

Chapter 4

5 What sort of evidence would you need to obtain in order to establish a positive relationship between child-rearing and parenting behaviour in the home and a child's academic performance at school? You need to produce a research design which would be comprehensive enough to account for the range of variables which might impinge on the home–school relationship.

6 What do you understand by Bourdieu's key concepts of 'habitus' and 'cultural capital'? Can you illustrate these with any examples and experiences of your own or from among your colleagues?

7 Bernstein's theory of language codes is frequently misunderstood and misrepresented. Its full scope relates aspects of social and economic structure to patterns of achievement and performance in school. Can you reconstruct the argument which links the two via the family?

Chapter 5

8 Stanworth's study of sixth formers' experiences of teaching and learning illustrates a very powerful gender effect in teacher–pupil interactions. Can you identify this in your own institution? A simple questionnaire to students and teachers and some straightforward recording of patterns of teacher-student interaction should provide you with the necessary data. This could form the basis of a manageable class project.

9 Using Bernstein's concepts of the 'collection code' and the 'integrated code', examine the structure and organisation of the curriculum in your own institution. What is the relationship between subjects? What is the relationship between teacher and taught in the learning process? Who controls the learning process (content, pace and method)? How is the knowledge assessed? This exercise can usefully be approached as a group discussion.

10 How is the organisation and grouping of pupils for teaching purposes related to the emergence of pro- and anti-school sub-cultures? (You should refer to the work of Lacey, Hargreaves and Ball.) Can you identify any such processes in your own institution?

General

11 How does the political process of comprehensive reorganisation relate, if at all, to the concept of 'equality of opportunity' through education? Remember 'equality of opportunity' can be defined in different ways.

12 How would you categorise and describe the main concerns and issues in British sociology of education since 1945?

13 What are the main differences in empirical emphasis and theoretical orientation between 'macro' and 'micro' perspectives in the sociology of education? How would you summarise and evaluate the main points of tension between the two perspectives? How would researchers from the two perspectives address the issues of: (1) classroom violence, and (2) progressive primary schooling?

References

Althusser, L., 'Ideology and ideological state apparatuses', in Cosin, B.R. (ed.), *Education, Structure and Society*, Penguin, Harmondsworth, 1972.

Anyon, J., 'Ideology and United States history textbooks', *Harvard Educational Review*, 1979 49(3) pp.361–86.

Ball, S.J., *Beachside Comprehensive*, Cambridge University Press, Cambridge, 1981.

Banks, O., *The Sociology of Education*, Batsford, London, 1971.

Bernstein, B., *Class, Codes and Control Vol 1*, Paladin, London, 1973.

Bourdieu, P. and Passeron, J., *Representation in Education, Society and Culture*, Sage, London, 1977.

Coleman, J. S., *Report on Equality of Educational Opportunity*, Department of Health, Education and Welfare, US Government Printing Office, Washington, 1966.

Cooper, B., *Bernstein's Codes: A classroom study*, Occasional Paper No. 6 Education Area, University of Sussex, 1976.

Douglas, J.W.B., *et al.*, *The Home and the School*, MacGibbon and Kee, London, 1964.

Durkheim, E., *Moral Education* (translated by Wilson, E.K. and Schnurer, H.), The Free Press, New York, 1925/1961.

Eysenck, H.J. versus Kamin, L., *Intelligence: the battle for the mind*, Pan, London, 1981.

Hargreaves, A., 'The significance of classroom coping strategies', in Hargreaves, A., and Woods, P. (eds.), *Classroom and Staffrooms*, Open University Press, Milton Keynes, 1984.

Hargreaves, D.H., *Social Relations in a Secondary School*, Routledge and Kegan Paul, London, 1967.

Jackson, B., *Streaming: an eduction system in miniature*, Routledge and Kegan Paul, London, 1964.

Jencks, C., *et al.*, *Inequality: a reassessment of the effect of family and schooling in America*, Allen Lane, London, 1972.

Kahl, J.A., 'Some measurements of achievement orientation', *American Journal of Sociology*, 1965, 70(6). pp 669–81.

Lockwood, D., 'Some remarks on "The Social System"', in Demerath, N.J. and Peterson, R.A. (eds.), *System, Change and Conflict*, The Free Press, New York, 1956.

Merton, R.K., *Social Theory and Social Structures*, The Free Press, New York, 1957.

Measor, L., and Woods, P., *Changing Schools*, Open University Press, Milton Keynes, 1984.

Reynolds, D., 'The delinquent school', in Hammersley, M., and Woods, P. (eds.) *The Process of Schooling*, Routledge and Kegan Paul, London, 1976.

Rutter, M., *et al.*, *Fifteen Thousand Hours: secondary schools and their effects on children*, Open Books, London, 1979.

Sharp, R., and Green, A., *Education and Social Control*, Routledge and Kegan Paul, London, 1975.

Stanworth, M., *Gender and Schooling*, Hutchinson, London, 1983.

Willis, P., *Learning to Labour*, Saxon House, Farnborough, 1977.

Woods, P., *The Divided School*, Routledge and Kegan Paul, London, 1979.

Young, M.F.D. (ed.), *Knowledge and Control*, Collier–Macmillan, London, 1971.

Further reading

Ahier, J. and Flude, M., (ed.), *Contemporary Education Policy*, Croom Helm, London, 1983.

Apple, M., *Ideology and Curriculum*, Routledge and Kegan Paul, London, 1979.

Ball, S.J. (ed.), *Comprehensive Schooling: A Reader*, Falmer Press, Lewes, 1984.

Bash, L., Coulby, D. and Jones, C., *Urban Schooling*, Holt, Rinehart and Winston, Eastbourne, 1985.

Burgess, R.G. (ed.), *The Research Process in Educational Settings: Ten Case Studies*, Falmer Press, Lewes, 1984.

Davies, L., *Pupil Power: Deviance and Gender in School*, Falmer Press, Lewes, 1984.

Hargreaves, D.H., *The Challenge for the Comprehensive School*, Routledge and Kegan Paul, London, 1982.

Tierney, J. (ed.), *Race, Migration and Schooling*, Holt, Rinehart and Winston, Eastbourne, 1982.

Walker, S. and Barton, L. (eds.), *Gender, Class and Education*, Falmer Press, Lewes, 1983.

Whitty, G., *Sociology and School Knowledge*, Methuen, London, 1985.

Woods, P.E., *Sociology and the School*, Routledge and Kegan Paul, London, 1983.

Index